WHY BAD THINGS HAPPEN TO GOOD PEOPLE

(The Christian's Promised Land)

A 2 Peter 1:5 study

by Mark D. Bristow

xulon
PRESS

ACKNOWLEDGEMENTS

Throughout the entire course of my life, in which this work was created, I have given thanks and glory to God our Father and Jesus Christ our big brother. I hope that it is understood by all that He really is the author and our gratitude, corporately, is due Him.

I would, however, be remiss if I failed to mention some of our fellow residents on this planet for their contributions to seeing this work completed.

My Dad. He has done so much, for my family and me, that it allowed me to focus much less on day-to-day requirements and stay deep in study and prayer. If ever there was a hero in the natural sense of the word, it is he.

My Step-Dad. Grammar is not my strong point, as you will soon see. I write as I speak. He took my general conversation piece and turned it into a better-written format. Had I used all of his suggestions, this would have been a well-written book by all grammatical standards. Trouble is, it didn't sound like me when I read it. So if the grammar of this book disturbs you, Joe did his best to fix that. Don't blame him!

My Sister and Nephew. They read the rough draft for me and I received incomparable insight and criticism. Having a background in the sciences and math, I tend to think that everyone makes the same connections I make. They proved that I couldn't make that assumption. That is something I never would have found without them.

My friend Jim. He also read the rough draft. Being a student of the Word, and an entrant into seminary, he viewed it from a more than casual perspective. His list of items for critique was very important to me. It made me think on an entirely different level to help get the necessary message across to the most people possible. Although I do not believe for an instant that every reader will find this work easily digestible and incorporated into their lives, I can certainly say that many more will be able to do so, thanks to Jim.

CONTENTS

Introduction...ix

One   God-Speak.................................11

Two   God Does Not Lie 19

Three   Promise of a Land 27

Four   Entering the Land........................35

Five   Failure No Excuse.......................43

Six   Jump to Jesus 49

Seven   Preach This Message....................57

             Kingdom of God 69

             Not Just the Twelve.....................73

Eight   Four - Six - Two 79

Nine   Enemies of Man 89

Ten   Treaties....................................97

Eleven   To Train in Warfare 111

INTRODUCTION

B ooks of this sort are easier to write than to accept into public knowledge. Foremost in this "study guide" must be the understanding that this work is based entirely on the Holy Bible as a reference. Frequently throughout will be excerpts from the HOLY BIBLE, NEW INTERNATIONAL VERSION. Thus anyone may follow along as conclusions are drawn. Make no mistake; conclusions drawn are not merely from a logical perspective, but from revealed knowledge and years of prayer.

To follow these conclusions the reader must understand the relationship of the Old Testament to the New Testament. Yes, scholars of every type can list you hundreds of differing relationships between the testaments, but the one most commonly observed, if not definitively expressed, is the concept that the Old Testament provides a foreshadowing or an "archetype" of that which was to be fulfilled by the New Testament, and in specific, the Christ, Jesus of

Nazareth. As a brief example, Paul explains this relationship when he preaches on the concept of the promise to Abraham of having been made to his 'seed' (singular) not 'seeds' plural. [Galatians 3:16] Many will bring to light the incident of the covenant cutting between "Abram" and God. As you may recall, Abraham was asleep during the covenant making; yet two members participated. [Genesis 15:12-18] This is widely accepted as being a covenant cut between God the Father and Jesus the Son. Hence, the covenant of Abraham becomes the foreshadowing of the covenant between Father and Son.

The final idea that we must have before we embark on this study is that the Holy Bible is the Word of God. If for any reason you determine that you cannot accept this particular position, then this book will be very boring reading. But for those whose hearts seek the Truth of God's Word, and in it place their delight, this book will open your eyes to a vast amount of knowledge. Much that goes on in the "church" today will be readily understood. With this book, and the books due to follow, we will learn so much about Jesus and His intent that we cannot fail to be better equipped to serve people around us. Finally, you will be able to explain to loved ones *why bad things happen to good people.*

ONE

GOD-SPEAK

Communication is a two-way street. In order for me to transfer a concept over to you, we both have to understand the meaning and value of the words being used. If I understand the words to mean one thing, and you understand them to mean another, then we can talk all day long and never communicate. So the beauty of life is when we actually do understand things on the same plane.

Wouldn't it be wonderful to have a full understanding of everything the Lord God has ever said, and ever will say? Perhaps someday we will, but we currently see as through a glass darkly. But one thing we <u>must</u> accept is this: When God speaks we may not know what He means. Simple enough? Let us evaluate this position before we continue.

Many debates have been sparked by the first chapter of Genesis, and rightfully so. I am not here to spur debate, but rather to illuminate the concept of our lack of understanding. Therefore please consider the passage from Genesis Chapter 1 verse 3 to verse 19.

And God said, "Let there be light," and there was light. God saw that the light was good, and he separated the light from the darkness. God called the light "day" and the darkness he called "night." And there was evening, and there was morning - the first day.

And God said, "Let there be an expanse between the waters to separate water from water." So God made the expanse and separated the water under the expanse from the water above it. And it was so. God called the expanse "sky." And there was evening, and there was morning - the second day.

And God said, "Let the water under the sky be gathered to one place, and let dry ground appear." And it was so. God called the dry ground "land," and the gathered waters, "seas." And God saw that it was good.

Then God said, "Let the land produce vegetation: seed-bearing plants and trees on the land that bear fruit according to their various kinds." And it was so. The land produced vegetation: plants bearing seed according to their kinds and trees bearing fruit with seed in it according to their kinds. And God saw that it was good. And there was evening, and there was morning - the third day.

And God said, "Let there be lights in the expanse of the sky to separate the day from the night, and let them serve as signs to mark seasons and days and years, and let them be lights in the expanse of the sky to give light on the earth." And it was so. God made two great lights - the greater light to govern the day and the lesser light to govern the night. He also made the stars. God set them in the expanse of the sky to give light on the earth, to govern the day and the night, and to separate light from darkness. And God saw that it was good. And there was evening, and there was morning - the fourth day.

Now please follow this brief summary.

Verse 3 - "Let there be light". Separated light from the darkness. Called the light "Day", and the darkness "Night". Day One.

Verse 6 - "Let there be an expanse between the waters to separate water from water." This expanse was called "Sky". Day Two.

Verse 9 - "Let the water under the sky be gathered to one place, and let dry ground appear." The dry ground was called "Land" and the gathered waters were called "seas". The land then produced vegetation: Plants bearing seed according to their kinds and trees bearing fruit with seed in it according to their kinds. Day Three.

Verse 14 - "Let there be lights in the expanse of the sky to separate the day from the night, and let them serve as signs to mark seasons and days and years, and let them be lights in the expanse of the sky to give light on the earth." One governs day, other governs night. We call them the Sun, Moon and Stars. Day Four.

Here is my point: What we call Day and Night were not even created until the fourth day! So, while God is creating the earth for the first three days, He is doing so without a Sun and Moon. Therefore, we *must* assert that we do not understand what God exactly means when He says "the first day..."

Perhaps this will help. Baseball. Everyone knows about baseball nowadays. Owners and players had their discord over money. Fans were only trickling back to games. Now records are being broken regularly, and history is being made. But if you ask the opinions of elderly baseball fans, you will find that the game was a much different game in say, Mickey Mantle's day. Note that "day". It wasn't a twenty-four hour period in which Mickey Mantle was one of the world's greatest baseball players. No, it was a specified, limited period of time—an era so to speak. "Mickey Mantle's day". Similarly we have all heard "granddad" talk about "...back in *my* day, we used to walk to school in six feet of snow with only a sweater..." That is not referencing a single day, so much as a given period. Hence, the creation story does not have to occur in six twenty-four hour time periods. It is much more likely that creation followed the example God gave in Isaiah. In the book of Isaiah, chapter 55 verses 10 and 11, God says, "As the rain and the snow come down from heaven, and do not return to it without watering the earth and making it bud and flourish, so that it yields seed for the sower and bread for the eater, so is my word that goes out from my mouth: It will not return to me empty, but will accomplish what I desire and achieve the purpose for which I sent it." Well, when the rain hits the earth, crops do not instantaneously spring up. It is a process. A process that has the beginning of moisture and earth. So also was creation. A process that had the beginning of God's spoken command. That command carried the power to perform, and the process immediately began, but was not an instantaneous appearance.

Another brief passage. Consider the curse on the serpent in Genesis Chapter 3 verse 15. God says, "And I will put enmity between you and the woman, and between your offspring and hers; he will crush your head, and you will strike his heel." Well, Adam and Eve proceeded to have more children. The three to whom we are introduced are Abel, Cain and Seth. None of these "offspring" of Eve crushed the head of the serpent (Satan). So there must be a different "he" to whom God is referring. Of course we now know that Jesus of Nazareth is the offspring spoken of, but at the time we wouldn't have known. We tend to think in terms of time. When God says "her offspring" we would think that her very next child should be the one. That is not how God sees things. Since God lives outside of time (i.e. eternity), He speaks of things without reference to time. So it is simply understood that referring to Jesus of Nazareth in this discourse is viable in respect to timelessness.

Finally, for this section, let us consider the Passover scenario. Exodus Chapter 12.

The LORD said to Moses and Aaron in Egypt, "This month is to be the first month of your year. Tell the whole community of Israel that on the tenth day of this month each man is to take a lamb for his family, one for each household. If any household is too small for a whole lamb, they must share one with their nearest neighbor, having taken into account the number of people there are. You are to determine the amount of lamb needed in accordance with what each person will eat. The animals you choose must be year old males without defect, and you may take them from the sheep or the goats. Take care of them until the fourteenth day of the month, when all the people of the community of Israel must slaughter them at twilight. Then they are to take some of the blood and put it on the sides and tops of the doorframes of the houses where they eat the lambs. That same night they are to eat the meat roasted over the fire along with bitter herbs, and bread made without yeast.

Do not eat the meat raw or cooked in
water, but roast it over the fire - head,
legs and inner parts. Do not leave any of
it until morning; if some is left till morning, you must burn it. This is how you are
to eat it: with your cloak tucked into your
belt, your sandals on your feet and your
staff in your hand. Eat it in haste; it is the
LORD's Passover. "

Now consider the case of the Lamb. The lamb of
the Passover was taken into the household and
befriended for four days. In the same way that it
would be difficult for us to imagine not loving a new
puppy in the home, so also was it difficult to not love
that lamb. Then, the lamb is brutally slaughtered and
eaten. Its blood is dipped and used to cover the doors
of the household, protecting the inhabitants from the
wrath of God throughout Egypt. Well, several
hundred years later, Jesus of Nazareth, the Lamb of
God, would do the same thing. He would be
befriended by the people of His day. And in short
order, He would be brutally slaughtered. His body
and blood would be eaten in the form of bread and
wine. And His blood would protect His people from
the wrath of God. This sacrifice of Himself took
away the sins of the world. No one reading the
Passover account would have imagined that one day
a man would actually be that lamb. This is a perfect
example of "God-speak".

Can we agree then that we may not always
understand, at first glance, precisely what the Lord

God means when He says something? Or that even though God means exactly what He says, we may not always be able to place the fulfillment on a time line? It is not always easy to differentiate between God's words when used as an immediate force, and when they are used as a promise of a future. If we will continue on with the basic assumption that God is true, then perhaps we will be able to learn how to make that differentiation. I think that would be a safe assumption upon which to continue. By holding tightly to this safe assumption, we will build in ourselves a foundation that may very well prepare us for fruitful communication with the Spirit of God.

TWO

GOD DOES NOT LIE

When my daughter Delaney was turning ten, she had seriously outgrown her bicycle. Although she had asked me for a new video game machine for her birthday, I had told her I would buy her a new bike instead. I spent several days, sporadically, shopping for a good bike that would fit her nicely. Yet every couple of days she would confront me. "Dad, I thought you were going to buy me a new bike?" After a handful of weeks went by, and I had narrowed the choices down somewhat, I was ready to take her shopping with me. (Dad does not shop well with daughter, trust me). As I was going to fetch Delaney to invite her to get her new bike, I overheard her telling a friend that she thinks Dad lied about the new bike. She played right in to the norms of society.

It is almost human nature to assume that those ideas with which we disagree, that we do not fully understand, or cannot see the completion of, are either lies or errors. It is rather well accepted as a theory. Just consider politics. When a politician says one thing and does another, we assume he was 'lying' from the start when in reality he may have been speaking truthfully, if not clearly. Lawyers are also well versed in this type of craftiness. Although they are not supposed to utter things known to be untruthful, they do have a way with distorting the facts to their own advantage. God is not like that. He speaks from beyond time, without the restraints of time. We must get to a condition where we do not consider the unknown to be false, or the unseen to be left undone. There is a necessity in this understanding. When God speaks He sets forth power to produce. You can review this with Isaiah Chapter 55 verses 8 through 11 concerning the power resident in the words God speaks.

> "For my thoughts are not your thoughts, neither are your ways my ways," declares the LORD. "As the heavens are higher than the earth, so are my ways higher than your ways and my thoughts than your thoughts. As the rain and the snow come down from heaven, and do not return to it without watering the earth and making it bud and flourish, so that it yields seed for the sower and bread for the eater, so is my word that goes out from my mouth: It will not return to me empty, but will accomplish what I desire and

achieve the purpose for which I sent it."

The mere condition of our inability to 'see' the results of His words is not to be considered grounds for determining the truthfulness of God. It is absolutely necessary to condition our selves to accept God's word as truth. This position is well earned, and it is further stated as such. Please consider Numbers Chapter 23 verse 19.

"God is not a man that he should lie, nor a son of man that he should change his mind. Does he speak and then not act? Does he promise and not fulfill?"

This is very important, if not crucial, to our understanding of why bad things happen to good people. Note the emphasis. "God is not a man that he should lie." He will not lie. Men lie. Often! Oh, most times it is a "white lie" to "protect someone's feelings", but it is a lie nonetheless. But we do not like to admit that we lie. Being human, we like to make excuses for our own 'misspoken' words. Perhaps we 'changed our minds'? "Nor a son of man that he should change his mind". He took that into consideration. No, He didn't change His mind. Then we have the tendency to judge His work. Thus He adds, "Does he speak and then not act?" He further develops His character by differentiating between the power of His mere words, and His deliberate intentions. He does this by distinguishing His promises. "Does he promise and not fulfill?" This difference is best seen by the creation event and the curse. In the creation, God spoke and there were immediate results. The process of creation began right away, as would the process of growing vegetation after the rain. In the curse (Gen 3) there comes the 'promise' of the offspring that would crush the serpent's head. There is no immediate result. Knowing this, and knowing frail humanity, God makes the distinction in Numbers 23 as we have seen. Therefore, having previously determined (in Chapter One) that it is quite possible that we may not completely understand just what God means, it becomes imperative that we rest upon this one concept that God is not a man that He should lie. If we read the Bible and come across something that seems not to make sense, or to contradict our understanding, then we return to Numbers 23:19. Our lack of understanding does not constitute a lie by God.

Our meager understanding of the ways of God tends to restrict our trust in His willingness, or capability, to fulfill His promises. But we are not alone! Please consider Abraham. Arguably one of the most important figures in the Bible, Abraham is the founding father of two nations of people: Ishmael and Isaac. The Arabs and the Jews. Yet how did Ishmael come to be? Consider Genesis Chapter 15 verses 4 and 5.

Then the word of the LORD came to him: "This man [Eliezer of Damascus] will not be your heir, but a son coming from your own body will be your heir." He took him outside and said, "Look up to the heavens and count the stars - if indeed you can count them." Then he said to him, "So shall your offspring be."

Here God promises to give Abram (soon to be Abraham) a son of his own and an offspring will surely result from that event. God even compares this expected family tree to the number of stars in the sky. Abram, being in his eighties and his wife being in her seventies, was nonetheless expectant to receive these offspring.

Well, being human as we all are, misunderstanding and impatience soon set in. In Genesis Chapter 16, Sarai, Abram's wife, got this idea that perhaps God meant that she could build a family through a "surrogate mother" - her handmaiden Hagar. Genesis 16: 1 and 2—

Now Sarai, Abram's wife, had borne him no children. But she had an Egyptian maidservant named Hagar; so she said to Abram, "The Lord has kept me from having children. Go, sleep with my maidservant; perhaps I can build a family through her."

Abram impregnated Hagar in an effort to fulfill God's promise. Listen, this is not so far-fetched! Men and women today are still trying to help God fulfill His promises. And every time we try to help out, we mess something up. So did Abram.

Look at Genesis Chapter 17. Abram is now ninety-nine years old and God "confirms" His covenant with Abram, changing his name to Abraham, and Sarai's name to Sarah. Abraham, faithful though he is, still is perplexed. He would just as soon have the Lord bless him through Ishmael [Hagar's son] as wait for another child to be born. Yet God is clear about this. Sarah will bear the son, and his name will be Isaac. Now God, being good and loving, says that He will bless Ishmael for Abraham's sake, but that, without a doubt, the promises God has made to Abraham will come about through the son of promise, Isaac. The Lord further restricts the wait on this idea by including the statement "by this time next year". So this has been a fifteen-year process. The promise of a son, the impatience and 'helping' God fulfill His promise, the confirmation of the original promise, and the fulfillment as originally intended. Yet we in our limited view would be inclined to have blamed God for failure early on in the process. As usual, when we do not see immediate results, we reckon error somewhere. Oftentimes, we fail to recognize the difference between the promise and the command.

One last example for this section. Noah. Please read Genesis Chapters 6 and 7 in their entirety. God calls Noah to build an ark to save a limited number of individuals and the animals of God's choice. How long do you think Noah was building that ark? He had no modern machinery. This ark was to be huge! Some preachers have stated that Noah worked 120 years on the ark. Not so, but not too far off. Certainly seventy years is not too far-fetched. How about fifty? Let me ask you this: Would you devote fifty years of your life building a huge boat on the idea that God is going to destroy the world by flood? Consider the way we are so impatient today. Can any of us truthfully commit to that project?

The point here is that several decades after God discussed the flood idea, the flood occurred. The average inhabitant of the earth did not believe this would happen, as evidenced by the fact that nobody else bothered to build a boat. Not even a life raft! Yet God's word was fulfilled accurately, and devastatingly. Since our goal is to understand why bad things happen to good people, and thus become better equipped to address crises, it becomes our responsibility to place our understanding in a position subordinate to the word or promise of God. After all, God is not a man that He should lie.

THREE

PROMISE OF A LAND

The overall focus of this book is to compare the promises of God concerning the Promised Land of Israel, and the condition achieved by Jesus the Messiah. Before we can do that with any accuracy, we need to have some degree of understanding and knowledge about the promises themselves, and how they brought Israel into their land.

How many centuries has Israel considered theirs to be the Land of Promise? And the Arab nations? Are they not engaged in the same old battles that were fought in the times of Moses and Joshua? And what significance is this to us? Let's take a deeper look at this.

The Promised Land is determined by numerous references to God's promises to Israel about the land of Canaan. It stems from God's promise to Abraham to give him all the land he surveyed. Thus the argument between Ishmael and Isaac. But this natural argument means nothing to us today. We have only one interest in the Promised Land, and that is found within the promises themselves. We will deal with several passages concerning these promises and the land.

Let's begin with Exodus Chapter 3. Israel is stuck in Egypt. God calls one man to deliver Israel: Moses. Verses 7 and 8—

"The LORD said, 'I have indeed seen the misery of my people in Egypt. I have heard them crying out because of their slave drivers, and I am concerned about their suffering. So I have come down to rescue them from the hand of the Egyptians and to bring them up out of that land into a good and spacious land, a land flowing with milk and honey - the home of the Amorites, Hittites, Perizzites, Canaanites, Hivites and Jebusites.'"

There are some very significant portions in this passage. Portions that we must have an understanding of before we can continue.

First and foremost, we must consider this passage from the "foreshadow" perspective. Israel is the "people of God". God's chosen ones. Egypt was the current world system and is used as an illustration of the world system today. So God intended (and still does) to save His people from the world system. Another major point is that God called one man. He didn't call a nation, or an army. He called Moses. Note that the Lord starts off by saying that He has seen and heard of Israel's condition. Many times we wonder if God sees our plight. He does. He says so right here. Further, He tells us WHY He has 'come down'. To rescue Israel and bring them out of Egypt and into their Promised Land. Three pieces: Rescue, bring out, bring in. Finally, their land is occupied by some people. They are the Amorites, Hittites, Perizzites, Canaanites, Hivites and Jebusites. Keep these names in mind for they shall become very important.

Let's look further along in Exodus 3 at verse 17.

"And I have promised to bring you up out of your misery in Egypt into the land of the Canaanites, Hittites, Amorites, Perizzites, Hivites, and Jebusites - a land flowing with milk and honey."

Break that part down. "I have promised..." When? Well, back in verses 7 and 8 if nowhere else. "...bring you up out...into..." Again, there is no 'swaying in the wind' here. God has a definite plan to complete. Up out of misery, into security and prosperity. And once again, here are our oft-repeated people groups: The Amorites, Hittites, Perizzites, Canaanites, Hivites, and Jebusites.

We are considering the promises of God concerning the land for Israel. Let's look at Exodus Chapter 23 verses 22 and 23.

"If you listen carefully to what he [an angel] says and do all that I say, I will be an enemy to your enemies and will oppose those who oppose you. My angel will go ahead of you and bring you into the land of the Amorites, Hittites, Perizzites, Canaanites, Hivites and Jebusites, and I will wipe them out."

That 'wipe them out' is devastating! The theme continues. Bring them out of Egypt (already performed by Chapter 23), bring them into the land, and wipe out the inhabitants, the six people groups continuously repeated. If you go further in Chapter 23, verse 24 says, "Do not bow down before their gods or worship them or follow their practices." This will reassert itself later.

Let's look at Exodus 33:2

"I will send an angel before you and drive out the Canaanites, Amorites, Hittites, Perizzites, Hivites and Jebusites."

Again, 'drive out' and the six people groups.

It is important to consider the repetition of these phrases. The promise of God cannot go unfulfilled or our initial assumption concerning the truthfulness of God comes into question. The specific repetition reinforces the commitment to the promise. But even more than that, it gives us slightly more insight into the character of God. There is one more Scripture passage concerning the promise that we must investigate before we begin to examine the "fulfillment" of the promise.

Exodus Chapter 34 verses 11 and 12.

"Obey what I command you today. I will drive out before you the Amorites, Canaanites, Hittites, Perizzites, Hivites and Jebusites. Be careful not to make a treaty with those who live in the land where you are going, or they will be a snare among you."

Here we are again. Preparing to enter the land of promise, God reinforces the concept of Him driving out the inhabitants. The same six groups as before. But now He adds a warning. No treaties! Verse 15 reemphasizes this. "Be careful not to make a treaty with those who live in the land." The difficulty in this passage is understanding the position of Israel. Whoever leads Israel, whether Moses or Joshua or any of the kings to come, stands in the place of God over the nations. If they make a treaty with a nation, then God Himself is at treaty with that nation. Thus, since the Lord God has promised to "wipe out" the inhabitants of the land for Israel it becomes imperative that Israel, under Joshua as we will see, not make any treaties with the inhabitants that will prevent the Lord from removing those peoples.

Time goes by. The Israelites receive the first portions of the Law. They arrive at the outskirts of the land and decide to send in twelve explorers to evaluate the situation. It was reported that the land truly was a fruitful land - flowing with milk and honey, but - that inevitable but - that the occupants of the land were large, powerful, numerous and the cities were fortified. Despite this report, two of the explorers remembered the promises of God. Caleb and Joshua by name. Caleb was absolutely certain that they could go in immediately and take the land. Joshua was like-minded, utterly convinced that the Lord, not the armies of Israel, would wipe out the peoples of the land.

As is usual, the ten explorers that spread fear triumphed over the two that tried to spread faith. It is in consequence of this fear mongering that Israel was condemned to wander in the wilderness for forty years waiting until the reporters of fear, and believers of fear, died and the innocent had repopulated the ranks of Israel. It is furthermore interesting to note that both Joshua and Caleb, although their position did not prevail, lived to enter the land at the end of the wandering. This is verified by Numbers Chapter 14 verses 29 and 30.

> "In this desert your bodies will fall - every one of you twenty years old or more who was counted in the census and who has grumbled against me. Not one of you will enter the land I swore with uplifted hand to make your home, except Caleb son of Jephunneh and Joshua son of Nun."

This passage is very significant! The 'nay sayers' will perish in the wilderness, but the 'faithful' will be preserved and brought into the promise. This is precisely the way it is today. As we will see in later chapters, the naysayers are still lost in today's wilderness of ceremony and tradition, and the faithful are going to be ushered into the Promised Land. It is this "Christian's promised land" that explains the concept of why bad things happen to good people, and provides for meeting the real needs of those who are suffering. Knowing the road map of promises that leads to the land is far different from actually traveling the road. Shall we walk together?

FOUR

ENTERING THE LAND

The time comes in everyone's life when it is necessary to step forward regardless of consequence. So it is in the Promised Land. It really doesn't matter what we have been through in our past, nor does it matter what awaits us in our future. Our hope rests upon that which we have learned to date, and whether that experience and knowledge will be sufficient for our tomorrows. Remembering that the Old Testament paints a picture of that which will be in the New Testament era, let us look at Israel's step forward as they prepare to enter the Promised Land. We will be looking in Deuteronomy for this.

Quickly look at Chapter 6 of Deuteronomy, verse 23. "But He brought us out from there [Egypt] to bring us in and give us the land that He promised on oath to our forefathers." Once again we see stipulated the reasoning behind the actions of the Lord. There is no hemming and hawing. There will be a conclusion to the promise of the Lord! Maybe there are some promises in your own life — promises that are taking more time to be fulfilled than you expected. There WILL be a conclusion to the promise of the Lord. Perhaps you have been subjected to the philosophies that try to denigrate the prophetic stature of the New Testament. There WILL be a conclusion to the promise of the Lord. Back to study:

Deuteronomy Chapter 7 verses 1 through 5—

"When the LORD your God brings you into the land you are entering to possess and drives out before you many nations - the Hittites, Girgashites, Amorites, Canaanites, Perizzites, Hivites and Jebusites, seven nations larger and stronger than you - and when the LORD your God has delivered them over to you and you have defeated them, then you must destroy them totally. Make no treaty with them, and show them no mercy. Do not give your daughters to their sons or take their daughters for your sons, for they will turn your sons away from following me to serve other gods, and the LORD's anger will burn against you and will quickly destroy you. This is what you are to do to them: Break down their altars, smash their sacred stones, cut down their Asherah poles and burn their idols in the fire."

There are some things we must recognize here. First, the 'when'. This is a certainty! "When the Lord..." is definitive. Notice also the inclusion of the Girgashites. We have continually seen the six people groups listed, but this time a seventh group is included. (We shall deal with this in later chapters.) Notice the command of utter destruction. That is an imperative in any man's life. When the time comes to leave the past behind and begin a new life, there must come that complete turn over or failure is sure to result. Finally, there comes the reiteration against treaties. Treaties will stop the Lord cold. He lists some subtle treaties that may be overlooked by a warrior group. How many of us would also overlook these easy treaties? Marrying the enemy? "Tolerating" their religious customs? Allowing their idols to stand? Those instances of 'failures to act' are just as viable a treaty as a written agreement between heads of state.

In Deuteronomy Chapter 20 verse 17 we see this again.

"Completely destroy them - the Hittites, Amorites, Canaanites, Perizzites, Hivites and Jebusites - as the LORD your God has commanded you."

It cannot be overemphasized that the plan for the Promised Land includes the courage to utterly destroy the inhabitants of the land. I want to once again remind you that the Old Testament accounts of this promise and its combativeness are archetypical of what will be real in the reign of Christ. It is necessary to learn, fundamentally, what is expected so that we can see more clearly the reality when we get to that point.

We come even closer to entering the land in the Book of Joshua. In Chapter 3 verse 10 of Joshua we read,

> "This is how you will know that the living God is among you and that he will certainly drive out before you the Canaanites, Hittites, Hivites, Perizzites, Girgashites, Amorites and Jebusites."

Again the Girgashites get a mention. That is okay. The real importance of this verse is the knowing. We've all done it. Wondered if God is in it with us. Wanted some way of knowing if He is helping us, leading us, teaching us. Well, for this event, the Lord God gives them a specific scene. Look at verses 11 through 13 of Joshua Chapter 3.

> "See, the ark of the covenant of the LORD of all the earth will go into the Jordan ahead of you. Now then, choose twelve men from the tribes of Israel, one from each tribe. As soon as the priests who carry the ark of the LORD - the LORD of all the earth - set foot in the Jordan, its waters flowing downstream will be cut off and stand up in a heap."

Pretty good sign wouldn't you say? Oh that it would always be so easy to tell that the Lord God was in it with us! Life would be a dream. Anxieties would be relics of ancient history. And fear? What could possibly instill fear in us if we knew without doubt that God was right in there with us?

Let's move to Joshua Chapter 9. Israel has begun the wars of Canaan. Jericho has fallen. Ai has fallen. Word has spread about Joshua and the armies of Israel. Look at verses 1 and 2.

"Now when all the kings west of the Jordan heard about these things - those in the hill country, in the western foothills, and along the entire coast of the Great Sea as far as Lebanon (the kings of the Hittites, Amorites, Canaanites, Perizzites, Hivites and Jebusites)- they came together to make war against Joshua and Israel."

I don't know about you, but I think that if I had heard about a very successful army's conquests, I would first consider peace treaties rather than warfare. But the Lord said that He would 'deliver' these nations into the hands of Israel. Thus they come together to fight Joshua.

Please notice the significance of verse 2—to fight against "Joshua and Israel". Once again, the Lord God is using one man to lead His people into His land of promise. Joshua, therefore, becomes a shadow of the Lord Jesus Christ. We will cover this in better detail later.

As long as we are here in Joshua Chapter 9, please notice the rest of the chapter. A group of people living in the land heard the stories of the conquests of Joshua and Israel, and they decided that a peace treaty was in order. They initiated a deception in order to facilitate this treaty, and it worked. Verse 14 of Joshua 9—

"The men of Israel sampled their provisions but did not inquire of the Lord. 15 - Then Joshua made a treaty of peace with them to let them live, and the leaders of the assembly ratified it by oath."

Verse 19 states that even after the leaders of Israel find out about the deception of the Gibeonites, they cannot allow the armies of Israel to attack them. As I mentioned previously, when the leader of Israel, who stands in the place of God, makes treaty, God is at treaty. Please remember this event for it will play an important role in later discussion.

Joshua Chapter 24 verses 11 and 12—

"Then you crossed the Jordan and came to Jericho. The citizens of Jericho fought against you, as did also the Amorites, Perizzites, Canaanites, Hittites, Girgashites, Hivites and Jebusites, but I gave them into your hands. I sent the hornet ahead of you, which drove them out before you - also the two Amorite kings.

You did not do it with your own sword and bow. So I gave you a land on which you did not toil and cities you did not build; and you live in them and eat from vineyards and olive groves that you did not plant."

This is a review of events to date. There has been much warfare, and the Lord is reminding the people that He has delivered the people groups into Israel's hands as He promised. Notice that He specifically mentions that it was not the warfare capability of Israel itself (not your own sword and bow) but rather the fulfillment of His promise to bring them into a land flowing with milk and honey. That same promise will deliver us into the Christian's Promised Land as well. The warfare recorded in the Bible demonstrates that this isn't a cakewalk. Things can get rough, and most likely will. We can doubt our travels and our guide. We can stumble along the way. Nevertheless, our stumbling does not change the path of the one who guides us. Trust the Guide.

FIVE

FAILURE NO EXCUSE

We are soon to begin the unveiling of the fore-shadowed events. Before this is practicable, we must consider a strong, yet well hidden, point.

I want to point out some errors on the side of Israel. I will list them rather quickly, but I want to encourage you to refresh your memory as to the exact events as listed. It should take you very little extra time to grab your Bible, turn to the referenced areas, and absorb the original message. Here we go:

Joshua Chapter 7. During the territorial wars, Achan pocketed some of the devoted items. This angered the Lord God and prevented the rapid destruction of Ai. If you will note verse 12, it is mentioned by God that this 'sin of Israel' has "made [them] liable to destruction". Also note that Achan is judged and sentenced for the commission of this sin. Afterward all is returned to normal between God and Israel and the promise's fulfillment is continued.

Joshua Chapter 9. The treaty with Gibeon. It shouldn't have happened, but it did. When the "leaders" of Israel realized their error, they knew they could not violate their treaty. Joshua then addressed the Gibeonites directly. The issue was settled by assigning a task to the Gibeonites for time immemorial. After this, the promise continues unabated.

Joshua Chapter 24. Presumes that some of the Israelites had kept some 'foreign gods' among them. Probably idol carvings and the like. This is not an end to the promise, but rather a time of settling. The inheritances are set out, and people bury their dead there. Clans are assigned areas and they continue battle to clear the land. Since God continues to prevail for Israel, the promise must be continuing as well.

Perhaps these small errors mean little to you, but it means much to me. You see, these display the concept that GOD IS NOT RELEASED FROM HIS PROMISES DUE TO THE MISBEHAVIOR OF THE PEOPLE. Many times we preachers today will say something to the effect that a person's behavior has prevented the Lord God from coming through for them in their lives. These examples definitely say differently.

Once more let us review our basic assumption for this study. Numbers Chapter 23 verse 19: "God is not a man that he should lie, nor a son of man, that he should change his mind. Does he speak and then not act? Does he promise and not fulfill?" The failures of the individual do not negate the promises of the Lord God. Individual failure, or sin, may make one open to destruction as is the case of Achan, but it does not affect the promise of God. One must have this thoroughly understood or the remainder of this study will hold little value.

Perhaps the best example of this concept, as it relates to the Promised Land, is the return of the explorers. As we have already seen, the explorers returned with two separate reports: One of fear - one of trust in God's ability to deliver on His promises. Rather than calling off the whole promise, the Lord God simply delayed the fulfillment until the faithless were out of the picture. God's promise went on, but those who chose not to believe it did not.

There are numerous examples not connected with the Promised Land that prove the validity of this point concerning God's commitment to His promises. Consider Samson. He committed adultery, dumped his wife and took up with Delilah. His "failures" did not prevent the spirit of the Lord from providing his extreme strength. Another is Jephthah, the son of a prostitute, driven away from his family. He became a deliverer of Israel.

It is important that we realize that our errors are not what prevent the Lord from operating in our lives. Perhaps it has more to do with our constant referral to our errors rather than to the promises of God? Nonetheless, we will soon see the clarity of the Promised Land, and we will know that our errors will not prevent God from working in and through us. However, that doesn't get us off the hook that is coming.

Please turn to the Book of Judges, Chapter 3 verse 1 through 6—

"These are the nations the LORD left to test all those Israelites who had not experienced any of the wars in Canaan (he did this only to teach warfare to the descendants of the Israelites who had not had previous battle experience): the five rulers of the Philistines, all the Canaanites, the Sidonians, and the Hivites living in the Lebanon mountains from Mount Baal Hermon to Lebo Hamath. They were left there to test the Israelites to see whether they would obey the LORD's commands, which he had given to their forefathers through Moses.

The Israelites lived among the Canaanites, Hittites, Amorites, Perizzites, Hivites and Jebusites. They took their daughters in marriage and gave their own daughters to their sons, and served their gods."

Classic treaties, but there is much more to see here. After all this talk about the delivering of the land, and peoples, into the hands of Israel; after all the years spent wandering in the wilderness awaiting the fulfillment of the promise of land; after the numerous referrals to trusting the Lord and follow-ing His commands, and how He would send His angel up ahead to clear the place out; after all of this, the Lord left these same people groups in the land to train the Israelites in warfare. Now this would be a cruel blow if we hadn't already learned about God-speak. It is only our human viewpoint that makes us believe that the Lord God had to drive out these peoples at this time to fulfill His intentions. We dealt with this human viewpoint in God-Speak. Once more, the Lord said He would completely drive out all these nations before Israel.

Well, did He? Nope. Says so right here. Why not? Because of Israel's failures? Israel's sins? Says here "...only to teach warfare to [those] who had not had previous battle experience." Who did He leave behind to perform this task? The Philistines, the Canaanites, the Sidonians and the Hivites. Where did the people of Israel reside? Among the Canaanites, Hittites, Amorites, Perizzites, Hivites and Jebusites. It is very important that we notice this format: Four categories of people, six specific people groups (tribes, if you will), two of which are specifically repeated. Again, four major categories, six groups, two were repeated. That is - four, six and two. This will re-exert itself in comparative analysis in Chapter 8. Before we can do that, we must look at what Jesus did in His ministry, so we have the other side of that comparison.

SIX

JUMP TO JESUS

The time finally comes to commence the fulfillment of the manifold promises of God. The
beginning, and end, of the promise's completion is
the Messiah. Now there have been many messiahs in
Jewish history, for the word simply means one
anointed to a position. But let us consider the word
"president". President can mean the top position in a
corporation, say, president of General Motors.
President can be the chosen leader of a club or social
organization like the Elks. But when we say, "The
President", the image of the President of the United
States of America comes to mind. So it is with
messiah. When one speaks of "The Messiah", one
speaks of the chosen, anointed one of God that will
usher in the fulfillment of the promises made by
God. As we in Christendom have come to know, the
individual who came to earth to occupy the position
of Messiah is Jesus of Nazareth.

It is the responsibility of Messiah Jesus to institute that that is necessary to complete the word of God. First in Himself, and then through His people. It is often overlooked that the authority of kings is a wide and sweeping power. For a king can 'authorize' the lowliest individual to perform a given task, and then that lowly one carries the weight of that king. So it is with Jesus. After showing the way by His personal performance, He then authorized His followers throughout history to do the same. Hold on to this idea.

I want to briefly touch on the fulfillment concept of the Messiah. The promises of God, being many and all based upon the Messiah, need to be addressed even if only at a glance. Let us begin with the easiest of these. In the Book of Isaiah, Chapter 9 verses 6 and 7, God promises that the Messiah would be human, and would bring with Him the sovereign reign of God.

> "For unto us a child is born, to us a son is given, and the government will be on his shoulders. And he will be called Wonderful Counselor, Mighty God, Everlasting Father, Prince of Peace. Of the increase of his government and peace there will be no end. He will reign on David's throne and over his kingdom, establishing and upholding it with justice and righteousness from that time on and forever. The zeal of the LORD Almighty will accomplish this."

Let's take this piece-by-piece. *A child is born.* Natural. Human. Not an angel, nor spirit, nor code, rule or law. *A son is given.* Male. Man. Many consider the "given" here to also refer to His sacrifice. If we were to delve into the promise given Abraham, concerning Isaac, then we would see the deliberate connection between the "sacrifice" Abraham was to make of Isaac, and Isaac's subsequent "return from the dead". Hence the extrapolation of "given" into "sacrificed". Fine. *Government on his shoulders.* He is and will uphold the government established by God. His Kingdom, if you will. *Wonderful Counselor, Mighty God, Everlasting Father, Prince of Peace.* There will be no distinguishing between God the Father, God the Son nor God the Holy Spirit, for Jesus refers to the Holy Spirit as another "Counselor" in the Gospel of John. The two (Father and Son) will be as one flesh. Seeing the one will be as seeing the other. For how can the Son be called the Father? Or He whom has called us His "brothers" be called Father? This verse reinforces the fact that the Father and the Son are one and inseparable. *Increase of His government.* He will expand His "jurisdiction" well beyond the scope of the mere king of Israel. *He will reign on David's throne.* Two things: 1. Must be a descendant of David. 2. Will be king over Israel as well as king over the nations. *The zeal of the Lord Almighty will accomplish this.* God's desire to fulfill all of His promises, and His excitement that the appointed time has finally arrived, will be more than enough to complete the task. There is very much said in this one passage, and it is culminated in the birth, life, death, resurrection and ascension of Jesus of Nazareth.

Because we need to thoroughly understand the relationship between the promise of God and the position of Messiah as fulfiller of the promises, let us look at another Scripture passage concerning the Messiah's duties. There is much use, if not misuse, of this next passage. Again, I am not here to spur debate, but rather to illustrate from Scripture. Please look at Isaiah Chapter 61 verses 1, 2 and 3.

> "The Spirit of the Sovereign LORD is on me, because the LORD has anointed me to preach good news to the poor. He has sent me to bind up the broken hearted, to proclaim freedom for the captives and release from darkness for the prisoners, to proclaim the year of the LORD's favor and the day of vengeance of our God, to comfort all who mourn, and provide for those who grieve in Zion - to bestow on them a crown of beauty instead of ashes, the oil of gladness instead of mourning, and a garment of praise instead of a spirit of despair. They will be called oaks of righteousness, a planting of the LORD for the display of His splendor."

This passage speaks of the Messiah to come, and the duties He will assume. Earlier I stated that the Messiah would "institute that that is necessary" to see that God's promises get fulfilled. This is true, but if you look at verse three you see the phrase 'garment of praise instead of a spirit of despair'. (We even have a song in church that speaks of a garment of praise for a spirit of heaviness. This is where that song came from.) But I must call your attention to a deliberate action taken by Jesus Himself that runs contrary to our understanding.

Please turn to the Gospel of Luke, Chapter 4 verses 18 through 21. [Jesus speaking],

"'The Spirit of the LORD is on me, because he has anointed me to preach good news to the poor. He has sent me to proclaim freedom for the prisoners and recovery of sight for the blind, to release the oppressed, to proclaim the year of the LORD's favor.' Then he rolled up the scroll, gave it back to the attendant and sat down. The eyes of everyone in the synagogue were fastened on him, and he began by saying to them, 'Today this scripture is fulfilled in your hearing.'"

Wow! There is a LOT here. First, He deliberately chooses this passage from Isaiah that absolutely everyone in all of Judaism knows is referencing the Messiah. Then He stops in the middle of a sentence! We just saw that Isaiah's Scripture said, "...the year of the Lord's favor and the day of vengeance of our God." Jesus leaves out the day of vengeance part. This is a deliberate act on the part of Jesus. This shows specifically that even when we think we have a good understanding of what God means when He says something, we may not see it clearly in relation to the time line.

Jesus sees this time relationship quite clearly. His first episode here with mankind is to perform the first section of duties. His next episode, soon to come, will complete this passage. That completion will result in the day of God's wrath and the comforting of God's people by bestowing upon them a garment of praise for their spirit of despair. If you look just a little bit closer, you will also see the relationship between God's favor and His wrath. For it is called the 'year' of the Lord's favor, and the 'day' of His wrath.

Now we have already seen that God does not always mean 365 days is a year, and 24 hours is a day, even as we ourselves do not hold to such measurements. The issue is that there will be a very long time of favor, and a rather short time of wrath.

Peter picks up on this concept when he states in Second Peter 3:8,9 –

> "But do not forget this one thing, dear friends: With the Lord a day is like a thousand years and a thousand years are like a day. The Lord is not slow in keeping his promise, as some understand slowness. He is patient with you, not wanting anyone to perish, but everyone to come to repentance."

Thus it is ever more evident that Jesus instituted the time of God's grace right now, and will institute the time of God's wrath at some time in the future. And this is not too far from our normal human standards. As parents, we hold our children in favor for great periods of time. Yet, when they are disobedient, or disrespectful, and warrant punishing, the "time" of our wrath (punishment) is very short in comparison. But right now, the duties and responsibilities of the Messiah and His subordinates are outlined by this shortened passage of Isaiah 61. It is a duty that blesses God the Father. A duty that benefits all of mankind. An absolutely necessary duty. Let's look into this duty.

SEVEN

PREACH THIS MESSAGE

Previously, I stated that the Lord Jesus showed the way with His personal performance, and then authorized His followers throughout history to do the same. Now is the time to investigate that position. The more we look into what Jesus said and did, the better we can understand His intentions. As with all communication, however, we need to get on the same plane. Perhaps for the next little while, you can come to my plane and see if we can relate?

I want to open with the fundamental reason for the Son of God coming to earth in the form of the human male, Jesus of Nazareth. The apostle John, in his first letter to his family of believers says, "The reason the Son of God appeared was to destroy the devil's work."

Now I know that we all have our favorite reasons for why Jesus came here, but the Scripture clearly states the above reason. Many like to choose Matthew

18:11 which says, "The Son of Man came to save what was lost." Fine, but that doesn't override the First John 3:8b testimony. As a matter of fact, when one considers the beginning and extent of the devil's work, then saving the lost becomes an action that destroys the devil's work.

Once again, consider the event in the Garden of Eden, where God is delivering the curses to the earth. The serpent, the devil, is cursed by the promise of the one who will crush his head, although the devil strikes his heel. At the point of this curse, the devil's work (deception of Man) has caused Man to be lost. But even more than that, the devil's work caused the ails of Man: Sickness, death, poverty, limitations, openness to demonic influence, submission to captivity. I am certain that deeper study could reveal more, but these are all that are necessary for our discussion. Thus, if the reason the Son of God appeared was to destroy the devil's work, and I submit to you that it is, then the Son of God must destroy those things that make Man sick, die, poor, limited, demonic, and captured by the various bonds that tie him. Into this we must also delve.

If we work on the assumption that John was correct, then we must be able to find a common theme that Jesus operated under. Easily found! Let us consider His parables.

Let's use Matthew 13, the parable of the sower, as our opening study. Matt 13: 1-9—

> That same day Jesus went out of the
> house and sat by the lake. Such large

crowds gathered around Him that He got into a boat and sat in it, while all the people stood on the shore. Then He told them many things in parables, saying: "A farmer went out to sow his seed. As he was scattering the seed, some fell along the path, and the birds came and ate it up. Some fell on rocky places, where it did not have much soil. It sprang up quickly, because the soil was shallow. But when the sun came up, the plants were scorched, and they withered because they had no root. Other seed fell among thorns, which grew up and choked the plants. Still other seed fell on good soil, where it produced a crop - a hundred, sixty or thirty times what was sown. He who has ears, let him hear."

The relating of the event of the farmer scattering his seeds on his field contains the fundamentals of understanding the differences in human understanding of God. It is a scattering, rather than a planting because the seed falls on various types of soil. The soil types determine the degree to which the seed can perform its designed purpose. In Matt 13:10-18, the disciples ask Jesus why He speaks to the people in parables. Jesus responds that prophecy demands that although the people hear quite plainly, and thus can easily make the connection between the example He gives and life itself, they are not hearing the direct answers to life's queries. Instead, this form of direct communication is "given" to the disciples. Thus, Jesus plainly explains the parable(s) to His disciples. Now, Matt 13:19-23 becomes important and relevant.

> "When anyone hears the **message of the kingdom** and does not understand it, the evil one comes and snatches away what was sown in his heart. This is the seed sown along the path. The one who received the seed that fell on rocky places is the man who hears the word and at once receives it with joy. But since he has no root, he lasts only a short time. When trouble or persecution comes because of the word, he quickly falls away. The one who received the seed that fell among the thorns is the man who hears the word, but the worries of this life and the deceitfulness of wealth choke it, making it unfruitful. But the one who received the seed on good soil is the man who hears the word and understands it. He produces a crop, yielding a hundred, sixty or thirty times what was sown." (Emphasis mine)

Many things need to be seen in this passage. First, notice the equating of "seed" with "message of the kingdom" or "word". By context, "word" is equivalent to "message of the kingdom". It is no different than our phrase of "pass the word". "The

big boss will be in today! Pass the word." Well, you
certainly wouldn't tell your workmate "word!" No,
you would say, "The big boss is coming in today."

Verses 22 and 23 discuss the remaining two soil
types, and the production value of good soil. In each,
the word of the kingdom is treated as seed sown. All
that remains is to determine just which kingdom
Jesus is referencing. Let's try His other parables.

Matt 6:33 "But seek first his kingdom..."
Matt 13:24 "...The kingdom of heaven is like..."
Matt 13:31 "...The kingdom of heaven is like..."
Matt 13:33 "...The kingdom of heaven is like..."
Matt 13:44 "The kingdom of heaven is like..."
Matt 13:47 "...the kingdom of heaven is like..."
Matt 18:1 "...Who is the greatest in the kingdom
   of heaven?"
Matt 18:23 "Therefore, the kingdom of heaven is
   like..."
Matt 19:12 "...the kingdom of heaven."
Matt 19:23 "...to enter the kingdom of heaven."
Matt 20:1 "For the kingdom of heaven is like..."
Matt 22:2 "The kingdom of heaven is like..."
Matt 25:1 "At that time the kingdom of heaven
   will be like..."
Matt 25:14 "Again, it [the kingdom of heaven]
   will be like..."

Now, if you would like to cross-reference all of
these to the other synoptic Gospels, simply equate
the 'kingdom of God' with the 'kingdom of heaven'.
You will notice that Mark and Luke spend a great

deal of time on the same theme.

So what is the essence of this message? Quite simply that WHEN WE ALLOW THE LORD GOD TO BE KING OVER OUR LIVES, THEN WE ARE IN A POSITION WHERE THE SON OF GOD CAN DESTROY THE WORKS OF THE DEVIL IN OUR LIVES, AND THROUGH US HE CAN WORK IN THE LIVES OF OTHERS. Let's take a brief look at some people who allowed the Lord God to be king in their lives.

Mark Chapter 1 verses 40 – 42—

"A man with leprosy came to him and begged him on his knees, 'If you are willing, you can make me clean.' Filled with compassion, Jesus reached out his hand and touched the man. 'I am willing,' he said. 'Be clean!' Immediately the leprosy left him and he was cured."

Please note that to this very day we have no "cure" for leprosy—except Jesus of course. This man came to Jesus, completely submitting himself (which is true worship) and accepting Him as "king" over himself. THAT is the Kingdom of God. More.

Mark Chapter 2. Verse 3—

"Some men came, bringing to him a paralytic, carried by the four of them."

Verse 5—

> "When Jesus saw their faith, he said to
> the paralytic, 'Son, your sins are
> forgiven.'"

Verses 9-12—

> "Which is easier: to say to the paralytic,
> 'Your sins are forgiven,' or to say, 'Get up,
> take your mat and walk'? But that you
> may know that the Son of Man has
> authority on earth to forgive sins....'" He
> said to the paralytic, "I tell you, get up,
> take your mat and go home." "He got up,
> took his mat and walked out in full view
> of them all."

As you can see, Jesus did two things in this
event. First and foremost, He equated the forgiveness of sins with the restoration of this man's whole
body. Secondly, He destroyed the devil's work in
this man's life. Also note the submission of the paralytic and the men who lowered him through the roof.
Whom do you think they accepted as "king" in their
lives? An abstract point needs to be mentioned -
when Jesus said, "Your sins are forgiven", the paralytic just stayed there. Why? He didn't understand
the relation between his healing and the forgiveness
of his sins. When one doesn't understand the "word"
the devil comes and immediately steals it away. But
the paralytic certainly understood "Get up, take your

mat and go home"! Jesus, by saying, "Which is easier to say" is definitively equating the two clauses. There can be no argument that He meant for us to equate forgiveness of sin with changes in our physical realm. This is not necessarily limited to personal sins, but also includes Adam's sins as well. In order to re-establish the link between God and man, Adam's sin must also be forgiven in our lives. Let's look at another.

Mark Chapter 5. This chapter relates the story of Legion. A man who was possessed by so many demons, that he lived among the tombs in tattered or no clothing and was so supernaturally strong that he could break the bonds of chain. Let's pick up this event in verse 6 and continue to verse 13.

> When he saw Jesus from a distance, he ran and fell on his knees in front of Him. He shouted at the top of his voice, "What do you want with me, Jesus, Son of the Most High God? Swear to God that you won't torture me!" For Jesus had said to him, "Come out of this man, you evil spirit!"
>
> Then Jesus asked him, "What is your name?"
>
> "My name is Legion," he replied, "for we are many." And he begged Jesus again and again not to send them out of the area.
>
> A large herd of pigs was feeding on the hillside. The demons begged Jesus,

"Send us among the pigs; allow us to go into them." He gave them permission, and the evil spirits came out and went into the pigs. The herd, about two thousand in number, rushed down the steep bank into the lake and were drowned.

So, Jesus drives the demons out of him, into a herd of pigs, and the herd runs into the lake and drowns. The man, however, was now in his right mind, dressed, and sitting with Jesus. There are some things that we need to realize here. First, Jesus did nothing in this vicinity except to deliver this one man. (The residents asked Him to leave, and He left) By driving out the legion of demons, He destroyed the devil's work in this man's life. Second, the pigs died. It is the desire of the devil to steal, kill and destroy. As soon as the demons were in mere animals, they were free to exercise their power of death. Notice how Jesus is absolutely unconcerned with the death of the pigs! They are <u>only</u> pigs! This *man* needed Him. This example is much more significant. For the man Legion did not seek Jesus, but rather Jesus sought him. The man, not being in his right mind, could not possibly accept Jesus as King. But what about those demons? Does not their fear and their words display that <u>they</u> know Jesus is the king? I should say so.

There are so many good examples of this concept that I cannot list them all. But I would be remiss if I did not include the following. Please read the account of John the Baptist's death in Matthew chapter 14—the entire chapter please. Allow me to recap. Herod beheads John Baptizer and John's disciples go tell Jesus. What happens? Does Jesus go raise John from the dead? No. Why not? Doesn't say. Let me add some small insight to this. This is war between Jesus and the devil. Destroy the devil's works. Okay, chalk up one skirmish for the devil. Now what counterattack does Jesus lead? Well, He withdraws for contemplation and the masses follow. First He heals all their sick. Then He feeds them with five loaves and two fish — approximately 12,500 people. Not over yet. He sends the disciples off by boat, and He prays until late at night or very early the next morning. Then He walks on the water. Not alone, He calls Peter out too! Not done yet! The boat docks and the people there recognize Jesus and He heals all their sick as well! Who won that fight? Did He or did He not destroy a whole bunch of the devil's works? Consider that a bit.

Need we continue with Jairus's daughter? The woman who was subject to bleeding for twelve years, and had already spent all of her money on doctors? How about the woman who was bent over for eighteen years? In all of these examples, people in trouble turned to Jesus as the messenger of the kingdom. By so doing, they accepted both He and the kingdom into their personal lives. My further point here is that Jesus, while preaching and teaching about the kingdom of God in the lives of men, was traveling the countryside destroying the devil's work in every category.

Let's consider this concept of destroying the devil's work. The devil inserted his role in the lives of men by deceit while in the Garden of Eden. When the Lord God returned to the Garden to visit with Adam, He displayed His awareness of this evil. Adam, not exercising his option of repentance, confession, and forgiveness, allowed a curse to be brought upon the land. This curse is the direct result of the devil's work. In the curse, God says that the one to come would 'crush' the devil's head. In the promises of the land, God says that the inhabitants of the land must be utterly destroyed or they would become a snare among them [the Israelites]. So the Lord God has said that complete and utter destruction of the 'enemy' is a necessity. Thus, the "One" who will fulfill all the promises of God must be a man of destruction. It seems difficult to equate the miracles and teachings of Jesus of Nazareth as destructive works, but they are if you consider what they are designed to destroy. We associate His healings with the love of God and the Spirit of Christ, and that is true, but if it weren't for the devil in the Garden of Eden, Man would not be subject to these. Therefore, these acts of love by which Jesus works many mighty miracles are works that destroy the results of that long ago garden event. However, my original statement involved the authorizing of His followers throughout history to do the same things He has done. Let's look at this aspect as well.

The fundamental Scripture that authorizes the believers to act as Jesus acted is Matthew chapter 10 verses 7 and 8.

"As you go, preach this message: 'The kingdom of heaven is near.' Heal the sick, raise the dead, cleanse those who have leprosy, drive out demons. Freely you have received, freely give." (Emphasis mine)

I call this the fundamental Scripture because of what it says, not because of to whom it is addressed. It is obvious to even the most casual observer that this Scripture is directed to the twelve disciples. But what it says is far more important.

Once again, it says, "...preach this message:..." Jesus is not sending them out there to tell about His greatness, nor to testify to what they have heard and seen. What message has He chosen? "The kingdom of heaven is near." If you ask many preachers today what message they think is most important to the masses, they will generally tell you that Jesus being the Christ, or Savior, is most important. For the most part, their choice will have something to do with 'believing in Jesus will result in the forgiveness of your sins, a right relationship with God, and you can go to heaven'.

Jesus chooses a different message. "The kingdom of heaven is near." Then, if you look, there is a period after that command. The next command from Jesus is this: Heal the sick, raise the dead, cleanse those who have leprosy, drive out demons.

This concept is reiterated in Luke Chapter 9 verses 1 and 2.

"When Jesus had called the Twelve together, he gave them power and authority to drive out all demons and to cure diseases, and he sent them out to preach the kingdom of God and to heal the sick."

He sent them out to preach the kingdom and expected them to heal the sick, drive out all demons and cure diseases. This is the assignment the Lord Jesus gave to His closest followers. We need a brief segue concerning the kingdom of God.

THE KINGDOM OF GOD

It is imperative that we understand the term "kingdom of God", or as Matthew consistently puts it, "kingdom of heaven". Failure to address this issue renders this study guide useless. So let's begin.

Jesus spends a vast portion of His ministry teaching parables concerning the kingdom of God. He also spends a brief time teaching about heaven and hell. It is necessary to point out that Jesus, by many examples, differentiates between heaven and the kingdom of heaven. The fact of the matter is this: Heaven is a LOCATION, and the "kingdom of heaven" in the parables is a CONDITION.

Can we equate this to salvation? When one accepts Jesus of Nazareth as the Messiah and places their trust in His finished work, then they are saved.

Have they moved? Are they physically different? No, but they are now in an entirely different condition than they were in before. So it is with the kingdom of God. If you consider any of the parables of Jesus that contain the phrase, "the kingdom of God is like..." then you must realize that He is speaking of a condition of your heart and mind, not the locale of heaven. If Jesus were truly speaking of heaven itself, He would have found it necessary to provide a bit more explanation.

Example: If heaven is a mustard seed, then we are going to be birds that lodge within. Forget the passage where Jesus specifically states that He is going away to build a home for us, a mansion if you will, for by the previous example we will be living in a bush. Perhaps another example will make it more obvious.

Consider the exhortation of Jesus that we should not worry about the necessities of life, but rather we should seek first His (God's) kingdom, then all the necessities that worry us will be added unto us. Well, if the kingdom of God were an actual location, then every time we begin to worry about our daily bread, we should drop everything and search for the kingdom of God.

Make this mental substitution: Kingdom of God = Atlantis. Now every time you tend to worry about your daily needs, stop and seek Atlantis. That's right, get yourself the most high tech submarine as yet unknown to man and search the depths of the Atlantic Ocean in hopes of finding a lost city of myth. So it must also be if the "kingdom of God" is actually heaven itself. Thank God it isn't!

Okay, how about some proof? If the first two examples didn't clench it for you, try this. In the Gospel of Mark, Chapter 12 a teacher of the law came and asked Jesus a question. Verse 28—

> One of the teachers of the law came and heard them debating. Noticing that Jesus had given them a good answer, he asked him, "Of all the commandments, which is most important?" The most important one," answered Jesus, "is this: 'Hear O Israel, the Lord our God, the Lord is one. Love the Lord your God with all your heart and with all your soul and with all your mind and with all your strength.' The second is this: 'Love your neighbor as yourself.' There is no commandment greater than these." "Well said, teacher," the man replied. "You are right in saying that God is one and there is no other but him. To love him with all your heart, with all your understanding and with all your strength, and to love your neighbor as yourself is more important than all burnt offerings and sacrifices." When Jesus saw that he had answered wisely, he said to him, "You are not far from the kingdom of God." And from then on no one dared ask him any more questions.

Please follow along as I review and paraphrase

here. A teacher of the law asks Jesus which commandment is the most important. Jesus answers that the oneness of God and the command to love Him whole-heartedly is the most important, and that to love your neighbor as yourself is second. The teacher of the law replies that Jesus is correct and expounds on this idea. When Jesus hears the wisdom of the teacher He says, "You are not far from the kingdom of God." Now listen folks, if the kingdom of God was a "place" like heaven is, and was located in Phoenix Arizona, then this teacher's wise reply would not have placed him a smidgen closer to Phoenix! You know it and I know it. Thus, if the kingdom of heaven is a location, then this teacher is not the least bit closer to the location simply because his heart is right. No friends, the kingdom of God is a heart condition. When you allow the word and ways and love of God to reign supreme in your life, then you are participating in the kingdom of God. In other words, He is your king. That is all that is meant by the kingdom of God. It is His sovereignty in your life, not His location or palaces.

Now take this concept and rerun it into some of the Scriptures we used previously and see if they make more sense. Consider the daily needs scenario. You begin to worry about what you will eat, what you will wear. Stop. Seek first that condition where you release your worries and rely entirely on the Lord God to be king of your life. Now, as you stop your worrying and begin your search for His 'sovereignty' all these things will be added unto you. How? By your king of course!

Now let's look at the mustard seed parable. If the condition where God rules and reigns in your heart exists even in so small an amount as a mustard seed, you can "plant it" and it will grow. What is that? Well, you can take that area where you allow God to rule and reign, and always allow Him to rule there, and eventually you will open up more areas in your life where you allow God to be king. So many in fact that your little mustard seed will seem as a tree!

If nothing else happens in the rest of this study guide, I hope that you at least come away with the reckoning that the kingdom of God is not a place, but rather a condition in your heart and mind.

NOT JUST THE TWELVE

All right, we have seen that Jesus commissioned the twelve to go out and preach a specific message: The kingdom of heaven is near. He expected them to then heal the sick, raise the dead, cleanse those who have leprosy, and drive out demons. We then spent a brief session on the kingdom of God so that we have a better understanding of the commission. Now we must realize that the commission given the twelve is the commission given us all. For starters, let us look at Luke Chapter 10.

Verse 1 -

"After this the Lord appointed seventy-two others and sent them two by two ahead of him into every town and place he was about to go."

Verse 8 through 11 -

"When you enter a town and are welcomed, eat whatever is set before you. Heal the sick who are there and tell them, 'The kingdom of God is near you.' But when you enter a town and are not welcomed, go into its streets and say, 'Even the dust of your town that sticks to our feet we wipe off against you. Yet be sure of this: The kingdom of God is near.'"

Consider a couple of quick points. First: Seventy-two others. Obviously not the twelve. Therefore the old line that certain powers were granted the Apostles and therefore no longer exist for us today is hogwash. Here, plainly 72 people who were not the twelve disciples were given the exact same authority as the twelve. In case this doesn't jump right out to get you, look at verse 17 of Luke Chapter 10.

"The seventy-two returned with joy and said, 'Lord even the demons submit to us in your name.'"

The initial authorization never specifically mentioned

driving out demons, but it is easy to overlook such details when you are discussing 'common knowledge' of the time. Furthermore, in verse 19 Jesus says,

"I have given you authority to trample on serpents and scorpions and to overcome all the power of the enemy; nothing will harm you."

Please allow me to remind you that the reason the Son of God appeared was to destroy the devil's works. Here Jesus specifically states that the power and authority He granted the seventy-two was to overcome (destroy) all the power of the enemy.

We need to consider Luke Chapter 9 verses 49 and 50. This is after the twelve have been commissioned, yet before the seventy-two were commissioned.

"Master," said John, "we saw a man driving out demons in your name and we tried to stop him, because he is not one of us." "Do not stop him, " Jesus said, "for whoever is not against you is for you."

There is an Old Testament foreshadowing of this type of event. Moses called the leaders of Israel together that the anointing on him may be passed on to them. It was, but there were a couple of leaders that were not present that also received the anointing of God. Joshua, jealous for Moses, asked that he stop these men from prophesying, but Moses said that he preferred that the Lord would put His spirit on *all* of them. (Numbers 11:26-30) Thus, in Luke, this foreshadow receives light. Jesus established the concept of commissioning, and it was not limited to direct connection, but to anyone who would believe in His Name. This is extremely significant.

We need to sit back and consider some things here. First, the apostles are NOT the only ones authorized by Jesus. I believe the previous passage displays that quite clearly. Second, no matter who He sent out by His kingdom authority, He sent them out to preach the kingdom of heaven is near - heal the sick, raise the dead, cleanse the lepers, drive out demons. Those two concepts go hand in hand.

My previous supposition was that Jesus authorized His followers throughout history. Well, to investigate that idea we need to look at Acts Chapter 8. Jesus has died, risen, ascended to heaven in the clouds, and the apostles and believers have received the Holy Spirit at Pentecost. A devoted man, well liked by all and known to be full of the Holy Spirit, the same as the apostles themselves, was 'ordained' by the apostles to help in some areas of the ministry. Philip by name. Well, Philip was out preaching in Samaria and performing so many miracles that the people paid close attention to all that he said. What do you think he was preaching? Acts 8:12 -

"But when they believed Philip as he preached the good news of the kingdom of God and the name of Jesus Christ..."

What did Philip do? He preached the kingdom of God under authority of Jesus of Nazareth, the Christ, and he healed the sick, drove out demons, and other 'miraculous' signs. This is not Philip the Apostle. This is the Philip commonly referred to as "The Evangelist".

The point I am driving at here is that Philip was not commissioned face to face with Jesus. Thus his authority came from an historical perspective. This is sensible considering Jesus Christ is the same yesterday, today and forever. [Hebrews 13:8] Because of disputes it would be counterproductive to consider the lives of the men of God in past decades. Men like Oral Roberts, D.L. Moody or Smith Wigglesworth, or women such as Aimee Semple McPherson or Kathryn Kuhlman. For those who accept these people as true representatives of Jesus in their time, then it is easier to understand that His authority extends to all generations.

Thus, in the face of dispute I will stand by the presumption that Jesus authorized His followers throughout history to perform the same service: Preach the kingdom of heaven is near. Heal the sick, raise the dead, cleanse those who have leprosy, drive out demons. When we get a firm hold on this, we also will resemble Philip in his historical commissioning.

EIGHT

FOUR - SIX - TWO

Comparative analysis requires a minimum of two items to compare and contrast. At the conclusion of Chapter 5, I mentioned this comparison would occur here in Chapter 8. We are just about ready for that.

It now becomes important to investigate Jesus Himself in terms of His concept of ministry. We have seen His devotion to the kingdom of God and to the promulgation of that message. We have seen that He authorized many to do the job. But what about Jesus Himself? Let's turn back to Matthew Chapter 10 verses 7 and 8.

> "As you go, preach this message: 'The kingdom of heaven is near.' Heal the sick, raise the dead, cleanse those who have leprosy, drive out demons. Freely you have received, freely give."

Jesus then continues to teach the disciples in the intricacies of ministry, especially as it applies to the kingdom of God. Then in Chapter 11 of Matthew we find the followers of John the Baptist questioning Jesus. Look at verse 1.

"After Jesus had finished instructing His twelve disciples, he went on from there to teach and preach in the towns of Galilee."

This is definitely after Jesus commissioned the twelve. Verses 2 and 3 -

"When John heard in prison what Christ was doing, he sent his disciples to ask him, 'Are you the one who was to come, or should we expect someone else?'"

John the Baptist, who had seen the Holy Spirit descend on Jesus as a dove, and remain upon Him, is now having doubts about the personage of Jesus. Why? Well, everyone in that time was taught that Messiah (Christ) would be this great warrior who would reconquer all the kingdoms and restore Israel to its rightful place as the nation of God Almighty. The Messiah would be the one who finally allowed all of Israel to inherit the Promised Land. Would finally eradicate all the enemies of Israel in the land. The Promise of God would come true through the Messiah. John is sitting in prison hearing reports of Jesus and cannot tie the two concepts together. He is still awaiting the conquering warrior that will restore Israel.

Now look at verses 4 and 5 -

"Jesus replied, 'Go back and report to John what you hear and see: The blind receive sight, the lame walk, those who have leprosy are cured, the deaf hear, the dead are raised, and the good news is preached to the poor.'"

We must examine this reply.

Foremost here we should recognize a problem. Jesus had just sent out the twelve with these instructions: Heal the sick, raise the dead, cleanse the lepers, drive out demons. Therefore, when John's disciples question Jesus, His reply *SHOULD* be: The sick are healed, dead are raised, lepers are cleansed, demons are driven out. In order to be consistent, that would have to be the reply. Jesus is certainly not in error. There must be something else going on. Let's look at it one more time, but this time in the "Bristow translation" - The blind are blind no more, the lame are lame no more, the unclean outcasts are no longer unclean and need not be cast out, the deaf are deaf no more, the dead are dead no more, the poor are poor no more (after all, good news to a poor man is prosperity). All of these fall under the categories of heal the sick, raise the dead, cleanse those who have leprosy, drive out demons.

This sets up a system of general headings and specific accomplishments. There are four general headings: Heal sick, raise dead, cleanse lepers, expel demons. There are six listed specific accomplishments: Blind see, lame walk, lepers cleansed, deaf hear, dead raised, poor prosper. Notice that two of the general categories are listed as specific accomplishments: Raise dead - dead are raised, cleanse lepers - lepers are cleansed. So here it is:

GENERAL	SPECIFIC
Heal the Sick	Blind See
Raise the Dead	Dead are Raised
Cleanse Lepers	Lepers are Cured
Drive out Demons	Lame Walk
	Deaf Hear
	Poor Prosper

Four, six and two. Four general categories, six specific results, two were repeated. Sound familiar? Let's recap the Promised Land. The Amorites, Hittites, Perizzites, Canaanites, Hivites and Jebusites. Yet, in Judges 3:1-6 we see that the Lord left certain groups in the land to train His people in the art of warfare. He left the Philistines, the Hivites, the Sidonians and the Canaanites. Israel then dwelt among the Amorites, Hittites, Canaanites, Perizzites, Hivites and Jebusites.

Here it is again:

GENERAL	**SPECIFIC**
Philistines	Amorites
Canaanites	Canaanites
Sidonians	Hittites
Hivites	Hivites
	Perizzites
	Jebusites

Four general, six specific, two were repeated.

I bring this up as a point to ponder. God did not deliver Israel into the Promised Land as would seem to be expected from those many promises, yet it is impossible for God to lie or change His mind. We spent some time proving that we may not always understand what God is saying, or the full meaning of what He says, yet God is true to His word. Furthermore, it is the duty of Messiah to fully institute the promises of the land, and we know that Jesus of Nazareth is in fact the Messiah. Therefore, it becomes the duty of Jesus to bring the "people of God" into the "promised land". I submit to you that He did just that! You see, He deliberately commissioned the believers with four general categories, and He deliberately used six examples of detailed accomplishments. It is not a coincidence that two of those were duplicates from the four general categories. If you recall, the Promised Land sometimes included the Girgashites among the inhabitants. I mentioned at the time that we would deal with that later. Now is that later. The Gospels hold many reports of miracles, and specific types are listed frequently. Blind seeing, lame walking, etc. Yet on only a few occasions is there a mention of the mute speaking. Although this is quite possibly a common occurrence, it only receives limited mention. Furthermore, Legion, the man of many demons, lived in the region where the Girgashites lived. Jesus went there to free the man, then left. He did so little in that region, that it only bore a small witness. So also in the Old Testament with the brief mention of the Girgashites. Contemplate that.

If that is not enough information to stir your mind in the concept of Jesus leading us into the Promised Land then this may. Once more, let's use Judges Chapter 3 for reference. Verses 1 and 2 -

"These are the nations the LORD left to test all those Israelites who had not experienced any of the wars of Canaan (he did this only to teach warfare to the descendants of the Israelites who had not had previous battle experience):"

The Lord deliberately left enemies in the land to train Israel in warfare. Obviously, the Lord considers warfare a necessary topic of study. Now, since this is a foreshadow of what the Lord Jesus will do, then we need to see if He left us any enemies to train us in warfare. Turn back to the New Testament.

There are many "assumables". First, we can 'assume' that the people the twelve and the seventy-two ministered to were "left by Jesus" for their training. But that is too easy. Consider a better assumable. In Mark Chapter 5, Jesus is asked to heal a dying girl. He agrees and heads off to her house. The crowds swarm him; yet one woman who had been subject to bleeding for twelve years and had exhausted her finances going to the doctors came from behind and touched His cloak. At that instant she was healed and He acknowledged that to her. The issue: Why not heal everyone in the crowd? He could have! Are we to assume that there was no one else in that crowd of onlookers that required His ministry? That's a stretch! Yet He took no time to minister to them there. Why not? Well, He had to leave some people for others to heal in His Name. Yes, this is an assumed theory. How about one with better proof? Let's consider the crippled man at the pool of Bethesda. John Chapter 5. Jesus is headed into Jerusalem for a feast of the Jews. Near the Sheep Gate is the pool of Bethesda. Verses 3 and 4 -

"Here a great number of disabled people used to lie - the blind, the lame, the para- lyzed - and they waited for the moving of the waters. From time to time an angel of the Lord would come down and stir up the waters. The first one into the pool

after each such disturbance would be cured of whatever disease he had."

This is a significant piece of information. Now when Jesus came by there, He saw a man that had been an invalid for thirty-eight years. His action? He asks the man if he would like to get well. Does that seem like a curious question to you? Well, the man replies, "Sir, I have no one to help me into the pool when the water is stirred. While I am trying to get in, someone else gets down ahead of me." Okay, it is time to put on your logic cap. Were there or were there not other people at the pool at this time? According to the man's response, there MUST HAVE BEEN more people there. Why? Well, here are some sample responses that take into consideration the assumption that he was alone:

1.   "Sir, no problem. I am the only one here. The next time the waters are stirred, I am guaranteed to be the first one in."
2.   "Sir, there isn't another stirring due for weeks. I'll have plenty of time to crawl to the edge, making my chances of being first more realistic."
3.   "As long as no one else shows up, I'll be fine. Think you could move me a little closer to the edge?"

You get the picture? If the man was not concerned about competition for the pool, he would have been plain about it, but as the facts appear, he was quite concerned about not being able to get in first. Well, let's move on.

Jesus says to the man, "Get up! Pick up your mat and walk." That did it. The man was healed. Then Jesus slipped away into the crowd. There is no evidence that He healed anyone else there. I submit that this is no accident. Let me give some thoughts on this matter as well:

1.   Had Jesus stayed to heal anyone else, the Scriptures would reflect that. They don't.
2.   Jesus could have put His hand into the water and stirred it. He could then wait until the first person got in and out. Then He could have stirred it again, repeating this action until all of Israel was healed. After all, His Name is above the angels. He did no such thing.
3.   The Pharisees were angry that this occurred on a Sabbath. They upbraided the healed man. There is no evidence that they accosted anyone else in the vicinity—further indication that Jesus healed no one else at the pool.

It is imperative to realize that Jesus deliberately left some people in their state of affliction. Not to say that some people could not, or should not, be ministered to, but rather that He was not going to personally minister to everyone. He intended, and still intends, to train His people in "warfare" by leaving enemies for us to fight. Enemies such as sickness, death, uncleanness, and demons. Victories over blindness, disabilities, poverty, etc.

If you still have trouble understanding the concept that Jesus deliberately left some people in their current condition, then consider the Gentiles. You see, the Lord had prophesied that Messiah would also heal the Gentiles, and bring them into the family of God. Yet Jesus specifically said that He was sent "only to the lost sheep of Israel." He refused to minister to a gentile woman whose daughter was suffering. It wasn't until she picked up His hint that permitted His ministry to be to the Israelites, on her behalf, that she received what she requested. Yet after Pentecost, the apostles were deliberately sent to the Gentiles. That alone is enough to show that Jesus left room for our training. Hence, the foreshadowing of Judges Chapter 3 arises. This time He left "spiritual" enemies in the "land" for us to learn warfare. Now if we will fight, He will utterly annihilate our enemies. God the Father will receive His just glory, and all of mankind will benefit from our obedience. As it is written, "May God arise, may his enemies be scattered."

NINE

ENEMIES OF MAN

W ell, Jesus left enemies in the land for us to train in combat against. I think the biggest trouble we run into in this area is defining what is, and what is not, an enemy. Think about it. Conservatives will swear up and down that Liberals are the enemy. The reverse is true as well. Fundamentalists think Pentecostals are the problem. I think we can all agree that Lawyers get a bad rap. Furthermore, it is not even enough to "know" the enemy. If you consider a chessboard, each side has eight pieces and eight pawns. The black players are the enemy to the white. But the strategy that determines the winner is the one that convinces the opponent to focus their efforts on a piece that is NOT the King. Chess pieces are enemies in the sense of the game, but it is not that much different from mankind having enemies in the spirit realm. Man <u>does</u> have enemies in the spirit realm. Their sole assignment is to steal from you, kill you, or destroy your life in whatever manner they can perform that best. Whether they make you sick, or attack your family and friends, makes no difference. They seek only to prevent you from enjoying life and abundance. They are not always successful, but they are always trying.

Bad things happen to everybody. Some people suffer more, some fewer, but many events occur to everyone. This book discusses the reasons why bad things happen to good people simply because everyone has their own ideas of why bad things happen to bad people. It is amazing how we can hold some people in such contempt that we "expect" disaster to accompany their lives. When trouble comes their way, we rationalize it as their "just desserts" or as "pay back" for all the bad deeds of their lives. This is hogwash and it needs to stop today! For the Lord Jesus Himself made mention of that type of thinking when He said in Luke 13:1-5 -

> Now there were some present at that time who told Jesus about the Galileans whose blood Pilate had mixed with their sacrifices. Jesus answered, "Do you think that these Galileans were worse sinners than all the other Galileans because they suffered this way? I tell you, no! But unless you repent, you too will all perish. Or those eighteen who died when the tower in Siloam fell on them - do you think they were more guilty than all the others living in Jerusalem? I tell you, no!

But unless you repent, you too will all perish."

And yet, by contrast, there is the tale of the man born blind. Please pick this up at John chapter 9 verse 2.

His disciples asked him, "Rabbi, who sinned, this man or his parents, that he was born blind?" "Neither this man nor his parents sinned," said Jesus, "but this happened so that the work of God might be displayed in his life."

A point of interest to consider here: The disciples equated sin with physical adversity as cause and effect. Not necessarily so, although not a stretch. What the disciples failed to discern was Adam's sin. When Adam failed in the garden, the rotten effects of sin entered into humanity. These also must be conquered. Thus Jesus's statement raises issues. Many people I have talked to simply do not see the sensible approach to this Scripture. What Jesus said, in effect, is that the man's blindness was not the result of the man's sin, nor his parent's sin. Otherwise, Jesus was labeling three more humans as having lived sinlessly. Therefore this is the result of Adam's sin, and there is only one solution - display the work of God in his life.

This brings up yet another common argument. So let me begin with this: NO, the work of God in his life was NOT the blindness! If that were the case, then when Jesus healed him, He would have been countermanding God! So, what was the work of God displayed in his life? The *healing* of his blindness! So here we have two different cases: One where Jesus will not allow His followers to minimize the travails of people, and one where He does not allow His followers to assume the worst about an afflicted person.

This does serve to emphasize the troubles of "good" people. For the same ones that minimize the traumas of the socially undesirable, cry and wail when the socially upright fall into despair. How many times have you heard it yourself? "Why would that happen to such a sweet little old grandma?" Or, "Oh and he was so gentle, so giving. I can't understand why such a fate would befall him." Our limited understanding places us in these questioning positions all the time. Fortunately, we now can expand our understanding. For the whole idea behind this is one of motivation! When your heart hurts because of the troubles you see happening to the "righteous", that is your signal! Do you not know that "compassion" means "that burning in your belly" that makes you want to DO something? So when faced by the trials of the upright, your compassion should stir you to action! And what action should it be? Well, that depends on the trial. But it should always fall into the categories of: heal the sick, raise the dead, cleanse the lepers, drive out demons. The four, six, and two. Think about it. If God cannot get you motivated when bad things happen to good people, how will He ever get you riled up when bad things happen to bad people? Would you really minister healing to a mass murderer if he was sick? Would you minister deliverance to an alcoholic next door who abused his wife and kids in your presence? Perhaps in that scenario, but if that same alcoholic was hit by a truck, wouldn't the back of your mind wrongly say, "He deserved it"? It would be very difficult for you to motivate to heal him. Since that motivation would be shallow, how can God use it as "training in warfare"? Are we not surrendering to our own imaginations? Does that not qualify as "leaning upon our own understanding"? [Proverbs 3:5] If Jesus would heal anyone, why would we "rate" them by need? If Jesus would not condemn the well-known social outcasts (Galileans in the previous Scripture example) why then would we? We are ambassadors of Christ. Messengers of the Kingdom of God. Do we have the right to say, "No, Lord, I will not minister to him"? Of course not! Yet by holding internal bias against those we deem unworthy, we are in actuality rebuking God. Can that be done and ministry remain? Certainly not. Yet it is a common occurrence. Consider that a while.

We must recap the basic conclusion of this study guide: That the "promised land" is not so much the real estate known as Israel, but is rather the condition where mere men operate as ambassadors of the "kingdom of God" here on the earth. Using this conclusion, and the basis established in the Book of Judges, then we will realize that Jesus of Nazareth is our "Joshua" to lead us into the Promised Land.

Thus we must take note of the comparisons between the battles of Joshua and the battles of Jesus.

Can such a comparison be any easier? Joshua led his armies into battle. Natural, brutal, bloody battle. Jesus led His troops into battle also. Yet the fight was against sickness, disease, demons and fear. His battles were all won on the earthly plane, yet from a spiritual perspective. Even when mortal combat seemed appropriate, as in the case where Peter thought it best to fight against those sent to apprehend Jesus in the garden, Jesus would have no part in that. [John 18:10] Thus His whole focus is toward battling the spiritual enemies of man. Once again, let me remind you of Joshua Chapter 24 verse 12b - "You did not do it with your own sword and bow." As leader of the church, His duty remains to train us to fight the way He fought.

Do not let the idea that these battles occur on a spiritual plane confuse you. Paul the Apostle explains as much in Second Corinthians Chapter 10 verses 3, 4 and 5. He writes,

"For though we live in the world, we do not wage war as the world does. The weapons we fight with are not the weapons of the world. On the contrary, they have divine power to demolish strongholds. We demolish arguments and every pretension that sets itself up against the knowledge of God, and we take captive every thought to make it obedient to Christ."

Furthermore, in Ephesians Chapter 6 verse 12 Paul writes,

"For our struggle is not against flesh and blood, but against the rulers, against the authorities, against the powers of this dark world and against the spiritual forces of evil in the heavenly realms."

By these two brief passages, we see that Paul had an understanding that our battle was not to be on the natural plane, and neither would our weaponry. Paul was led into the Promised Land by Jesus, and that land was a condition of defeating the enemies of man in spiritual combat.

Can you imagine how little we would know about the Lord and His ways if He had eliminated sickness, disease, et al when He first appeared? No family, it was imperative for our training that He leave certain enemies in the land. But He didn't leave these enemies here to overpower us! No, we are to overpower them! As we examine the church of today, we must realize that we are not participating in such overcoming; at least, not in any grand measure. Perhaps it would behoove us to examine ourselves to see if anything is hindering us from performing at God's best? If there be any hindrances, then bad things will continue to happen to good people and we will be powerless to help.

TEN

TREATIES

Working on the conclusion that Jesus Christ of Nazareth ushered us into the Promised Land, then we need to answer some very vital questions: Why are we not operating in the miraculous as did He and the early church? What has come between God and us for the salvation of the hurting? How can we refine our connection to God to better serve others? How can we, as Hebrews puts it, "…let us throw off everything that hinders, and the sin that so easily entangles"?

To answer these questions, let's look at those things that seem preemptive to the Israelites entering their Promised Land. Return, please, to Exodus Chapter 34. God is making covenant to do the miraculous in front of Israel to provide them with the land. Then in verses 12 through 16 He warns –

"Be careful not to make a treaty with

those who live in the land where you are going, or they will be a snare among you. Break down their altars, smash their sacred stones and cut down their Asherah poles. Do not worship any other god, for the Lord, whose name is Jealous, is a jealous God. Be careful not to make a treaty with those who live in the land; for when they prostitute themselves to their gods and sacrifice to them, they will invite you and you will eat their sacrifices. And when you choose some of their daughters as wives for your sons and those daughters prostitute themselves to their gods, they will lead your sons to do the same."

Pretty good warning, wouldn't you agree? Let's take a brief look at it. "Be careful not to make a treaty...or they will become a snare among you." Please notice this. It does NOT say, "Don't make a treaty or I will not help you." Big difference. God is bound by His word, but people will not live in and by His word if they are bound in snares among the ungodly. Snares exist among us, but warnings exist as well. Consider this Scripture as fair warning. "Break down their altars..." Can someone please tell me how we can overlook this type of Scripture and build a notion called "Christian tolerance"? This is a destructive action.

We have seen that the reason Jesus came was to destroy the devil's work. So also should we. When we, as the Body of Christ, allow the ungodly to have an equal footing among us (be it "tolerance" or "respecting others beliefs") then we are not breaking altars and cutting down poles. Just another snare. "Do not worship any other god..." Do not submit yourself to any authority other than God's authority. Does that mean to rebel against the government? Well, Romans says that the government is established by God with His authority. So perhaps we need to consider this concept in more detail. In verses 15 and 16 of Exodus 34, God says that making a treaty with the enemy will result in our casual participation in their idolatries, and will eventually result in us training our children to follow their ways, not God's ways. Thus, by making treaties with the enemy, we are selling out our children's lives. A devastating possibility. Just what would be considered "casual" participation with spiritual enemies? Well, we have already discussed the treaties we make, but how about little things? Aspirin. Is that spiritual warfare? Doctor's in general. Are they among the list of those sent to strengthen the church? I don't think so.

Quickly turn to Ephesians chapter 4 verses 11-13.

"It was He who gave some to be apostles, some to be prophets, some to be evangelists, and some to be pastors and teachers, to prepare God's people for works of service, so that the body of Christ may be built up until we all reach unity in the faith and in the knowledge of the Son of God and become mature, attaining to the whole measure of the fullness of Christ."

I don't find doctors there, do you? Nor therapists, nor psychologists. These types of "professionals" so generally accepted into our midst are precisely that which is displayed in Scripture when God speaks of their daughters prostituting themselves to their gods and leading your sons to do the same. Casual participation. And if we read the rest of the Old Testament, we will see that Israel frequently surrendered to idolatrous behavior.

So now you may be thinking, "What has this to do with us? We didn't enter Palestine and make treaties with the inhabitants. We are innocent." Ha! Far from it family. Working on the conclusion that Jesus established us in the Promised Land, we need to see if we have made treaty with the enemies of that land. Once again, let us consider the four, six and two.

GENERAL	**SPECIFIC**
Heal the Sick	Blind See
<u>Raise the Dead</u>	<u>Dead are Raised</u>
<u>Cleanse Lepers</u>	<u>Lepers are Cured</u>
Drive out Demons	Lame Walk
	Deaf Hear
	Poor Prosper

Is it possible to take any, and every, listed condition and determine whether or not we have made treaty with the enemy?

Let's take the easy route by discussing the specific events.

The blind - Jesus opened their eyes. I'm not certain that that thought ever crosses our minds anymore. Perhaps we believe it beyond our ability. Perhaps we're "waiting on God to move" when all the while He's been way ahead waiting on us. So, what would constitute making treaty with "blindness"? Braille, white canes with red tips, seeing-eye dogs, computers that can turn printed words into audible words, government imposed non-discriminative hiring laws, to name a few. Not one of these truly helps the blind to see. The longer we tolerate such measures, the more we doom our children to missing the entry into the Promised Land.

What about raising the dead? Sounds outrageous to even consider it! Over the centuries, we have come to the conclusion that death is the just and final end of man. Once death occurs, our hands are tied. Jesus displayed, and His Apostles followed, that death is not necessarily a permanent situation. It is interesting to me, if not to you, that there are absolutely no reports by the New Testament writers of funeral services. None. It is easy to assume that deaths did occur, and some we know of, but there is nothing recorded in the New Testament about attending their services. What is heart wrenching to me, is our complete surrender to death as finality. Do we even bother to seek to destroy death? No, today we simply preach inspiring, tear-jerking, heart-felt sermons at graveside and hope that the remaining family members will accept Jesus as their Savior. Well folks, Jesus and the apostles only knew one graveside sermon. It was brief and to the point. It went something like this: "(Insert dead person's name or position) - Get up!" That was it. Jairus's daughter, Lazarus, the widow of Nain's son, Tabitha (Dorcas), the young man who fell asleep in the window as the Apostle Paul preached on into the night, even Paul himself after being stoned in Lystra. Although these people eventually died, they didn't remain dead in these individual instances. Nor should people today. Young or old, it doesn't matter. The widow's son is especially nice. Here is a funeral procession. Jesus interrupts this solemn occasion to knock on the casket and tell the young man to get up. Who among us has the intestinal fortitude to do that?! Well, if we don't get it, we are making treaty with death. We are saying, "Death, you go ahead and take those to whom you are not entitled, just allow us to preach tear-jerkers to the people." Consider that.

The lepers. Who thinks about it today? Leprosy itself is still incurable. But this goes further than that. It encompasses not only all skin disease, but those things which are of such disgust that people will not associate with those who have succumbed to the disease. May I offer AIDS into this category? It is incurable, and likely will remain incurable forever. When one acquires the disease, people are generally afraid to be around them. They become social outcasts, as did the lepers of Jesus's day. There is nothing that the learned community can do to change this. But WE are supposed to change this. Cleanse the lepers! Make them clean, meaning socially acceptable. And their acceptance will only accompany their being cured of the disease. But what do we do? Throw money at the problem! Establish places to ship the victims while they are being treated. Try everything and anything to see if it can help with the sickness. Establish government regulations about privacy and rights of those afflicted. When all along Jesus commissioned us to FIX IT. Unless we take the stance, and cleanse the lepers, we have lapsed into a treaty.

The lame. Jesus caused bodies that were malfunctioning to operate properly. What do we do for them? Do we heal them? Not often! No folks, we choose to develop life aids: Wheelchairs, prosthetics, crutches, etc. Although I am certain the recipient appreciates the design and intent, wouldn't the lame prefer healing? Don't get confused! The Living Bible, at one point, translates that the "lame" that Jesus was healing were missing body parts, and He restored them. Please keep in mind that I am not saying we should "do" these things, but rather that we should do what He said to do, and watch Him "do" these things as though through us. If you look at Joshua Chapter 24 verse 12b, you see Joshua speaking on behalf of the Lord God, recounting the events that occurred from the time the Lord called Moses to rescue His people out of Egypt, to the present. He says, "You did not do it with your own sword and bow." Well, the sense of this statement is that the people had personal knowledge of the hand-to-hand combat that actually took place, but the Lord was demonstrating that He was the true provider of victory. So also will it be for us when we step out and perform the miraculous to defeat the enemies of man. That is His design and plan, yet we cringe in terror for some reason. Truthfully, no one who wheels himself into church should wheel himself back out again. Yet it happens frequently in every type of congregation. Ah for the boldness of Joshua!

How about the deaf? Do we not see the treaties we make with the enemy in this area? Even within the walls of the congregation! Rather than following the Messiah and opening the ears of the deaf, we have people "sign" the sermons so the deaf can pay attention. To what consequence? Well, as long as the deaf are 'hearing' the sermon, why should the speaker bother listening to God to open their ears? And this is to the detriment of the afflicted, as it is to all of those we overlook because of our treaties. Furthermore, the totality of these failures to operate in the miraculous, result in the non-churchgoing public believing themselves justified in foregoing services. Now perhaps you LIKE to hear well-crafted sermons. Maybe you get a jolt from seeing a devout man of God preach at you every Sunday. Maybe you get a good feeling when a sinner or two gives their life to Jesus. What would happen in YOUR town if that preacher yanked a brother up out of his wheelchair? What if a traveling preacher showed up, stopped the sign language, opened the ears of every deaf member of your congregation, and went on preaching the Gospel? Which would have the more overwhelming effect? Which brings in two sinners and which brings in too many sinners to handle? We should be ashamed long enough to repent! Bless God that there is therefore now no condemnation for those who are in Christ Jesus!

What can be said about the poor? Today, we allow the government to practice socialism so that we are not responsible for the condition of the poor. Forgetting the fact that socialism is bad for America, how is it for people? If we presume, and I do, that the followers of Jesus of Nazareth are supposed to use their commission to help the poor to prosper, what type of cop out is it that we do not, but allow

the government to assist the poor? Do you not realize that your message, and your hands laid upon,
will do so much more for the prosperity of the poor
than free money from Washington?

Consider the lesson from James. James chapter 1
verse 27—

> **"Religion that God our Father accepts as
> pure and faultless is this: to look after
> orphans and widows in their distress and
> to keep oneself from being polluted by
> the world."**

Chapter 2 verses 15 and 16—

> **"Suppose a brother or sister is without
> clothes and daily food. If one of you says
> to him, 'Go, I wish you well; keep warm
> and well fed,' but does nothing about his
> physical needs, what good is it?"**

How can we continue to allow the government to
usurp our rightful place as it pertains to helping
those who have little or nothing? We cannot if we
ever hope to be used by the Lord in this area of
battle. His blessing, through your hands and the oil,
is all that a man needs to prosper (long term) in this
world. But if your heart is in treaty with the enemy
of the poor, then you cannot participate in the Lord's
work in their lives. Shoot, what am I saying? Treaty
with the poor. We have people *teaching* us to be
poor! That ain't a treaty! That's surrender!

Of all of these treaties, none is more despicable than our acceptance of mental anguish, or mental illness. We allow it to be a viable excuse for violent crime. We use it as reasoning for outlandish behavior. When in truth, it is impossible for a "mind" to be ill. I have heard a vast number of preachers say that demon possession is not what it used to be. They say that in the days of Jesus it was common, but it is very rare today. Rubbish! What is rare today is the realization that demonic influence, possession if you will, occurs all around us everyday. Yet we do nothing! Worse than that, we refuse to recognize it. Yes, I know that many have taken the concept to extremes, finding 'demons' behind every corner, and hiding in every bush, but that is almost preferable to refusing to acknowledge their effect on the human race.

Consider this: Jesus is preaching in the synagogue and a man stands up and says, "What do you want with us Jesus of Nazareth? Have you come to destroy us? I know who you are - the Holy One of God!" This man is described as having an "evil" or an "unclean" spirit. We call this demon possession, or demonic influence, but what is it? It is a man that inappropriately disturbed church to question the Lord's intent, and then he almost blew His cover by labeling Him the Holy One of God. But today we have exactly the same thing going on. Loosely moralled people all across our nation rise up against the "Religious Right" wondering if it is their desire to destroy "us". Those who hold to good religious teaching, and/or those who follow Jesus Christ, are a threat to the continued lifestyle of the ungodly. Why?

Because the ungodly are influenced by the demonic. The demons know that we are their tormentors and that we have absolute authority to make life decisions of their concern. Yet we do not. This is by far the worst treaty we allow. We even boast of it proudly. We are ignorant enough to call it "Christian tolerance". It is a devastating treaty that ties the hands of God in American lives. Is it because He cannot help? No, but as He warned us in Exodus, the treaties have become a snare for us and we have accepted their daughters for our sons, and given our daughters to their sons. Our "generations" are corrupted by our treaty. Again, shame alone should lead us to full-scale repentance. And if we cannot recognize these minor cases of demonic oppression, how can we possibly attack the major ones? How could we be willing to attack "multiple sclerosis" in the identity of the demonic? What about Alzheimer's disease? It probably never even occurred to you that these are not physical or mental malfunctions, but rather direct results from demonic interference. If we do not learn from the small fights, the big fights will trample us. The seven sons of Sceva (Acts chapter 19 verses 13-16) will attest to that!

You may argue as to the validity of these individually listed treaty types, but you cannot look at the state of the church today and deny that we have made such treaties. In any event, the results are the same: Our leaders are snared in these treaties and cannot get the job done. We must overcome this condition and restore the fullness of Christ to the body. Can it be done? Don't ask me, I'm not God. Scripture displays the possibility. When Joshua found out that the Gibeonites deceived him into making a treaty with them, he demanded that they become the slaves of Israel. Very well. It is time that we demand that sickness, death, uncleanness and the demonic become the slaves of the church. That blindness, lameness, etc. all submit themselves to the anointing of Jesus on His body. This is not as far-fetched an idea as one might initially believe. Neither do I believe I am being too extreme in mentioning it.

Consider just a few Scriptural references. Probably the most well known, is Saul's conversion. In the Book of Acts, chapter 9, Saul is apprehended by Jesus Christ. After Saul's vision, he is left blind. Jesus obviously had no qualms about using blindness as His slave. Saul, now called Paul, also has no qualms to use blindness for its effects. In Acts chapter 13, Paul and Barnabas have been summoned before the proconsul of Paphos because the proconsul is interested in hearing the word of the Lord. Elymas the sorcerer opposes them in hopes that the proconsul will not become a Christian. (Incidentally, it reminds me of the demons worrying if Christ has come to torment them). Anyway, Paul rebukes the sorcerer and saddles him with blindness "for a time". (Acts 13:11) Let me make just a few more references.

Consider Elisha. He called down blindness on his enemies and God blinded them. (2 Kings 6:18) In 2 Kings 5:27 Elisha commands the leprosy of Naaman the Syrian to cling to Gehazi and his descendants forever. Elisha obviously knows how to use his enemies as slaves.

In Acts chapter 5, Ananias and Sapphira agree to test the Holy Spirit by lying to Peter. They drop dead at his feet. I reckon the Holy Ghost has no trouble with that.

Should we also consider the archangel Gabriel? In Luke 1:20, Gabriel commands that Zechariah the priest be mute until the birth of John the Baptist. I would have to conclude that it doesn't bother God much to use these types of temporary maladies for their deeply felt effect. I further believe that this is ample evidence that we should learn to be so bold. Perhaps even beyond enslaving the enemies of man, negating previous treaties may actually be better. Maybe if we repent, the Lord God will allow us to declare all previous treaties null and void, and we can start afresh? What harm would there be in asking? Might I hereby make this suggestion: That we approach the Lord our God in requesting that He invalidate all our previous treaties and teach us to stand strong and courageous in the face of the enemy.

May we all be forgiven for our participation, regardless of how unknowingly, for we continue to allow bad things to happen to good people. May we realize the strength of our opposition as we determine in our own selves whether to move onward toward Jesus, or remain in our current condition. Finally, may God help us powerfully should we decide to come closer to Him for this training.

ELEVEN

TO TRAIN IN WARFARE

If you have turned the page, may I assume that you believe you would rather be trained to destroy the devil's works, than to watch as others learn for themselves? It is a big decision that should not be entered into lightly. Perhaps it has hit you the same way it hit me? I sure hope so!

Having come this far, we cannot turn a blind eye to the truth of God's Word. To simply disregard it now would be irresponsible. So just where <u>does</u> our responsibility lie? Well, we need to meditate the "why" of this book. Judges Chapter 3 verse 2 says that the Lord God left certain warrior groups in the Promised Land to train in warfare those Israelites who had not had previous battle experience. We have thus come to the conclusion that the Lord God left sickness, death, demons, and leprosy (socially unacceptable, incurable diseases) in our promised land to train in combat those of us who have not yet performed in battle. If you do not accept that as a conclusion to the previous chapters, then at least use that as an operating assumption for this chapter. That is what we shall do.

The remainder of the Book of Judges deals with the ways, and leaders, that God used to defeat the enemies of Israel in the land of Canaan. Perhaps then we must begin to realize that the Lord God, through Jesus Christ of Nazareth, will raise up "leaders" among us that will defeat the enemies of man. Once again, this will not be a natural fight as Jesus's own ministry was not a natural fight. God does not expect us to physically attack sick people, or demon oppressed people, but rather to minister to them the same way Jesus did. It is not up for argument that Jesus battled in spirit. Neither is it up for debate that He commissioned His followers to battle as well. And it should be re-emphasized that this will be a supernatural battle. God is not going to raise up a doctor that finds a cure for a disease. Nor an entrepreneur who will eliminate poverty. Nor an engineer that will make a machine that prevents death. Therefore, we must take it upon ourselves to learn to fight the enemies of man and continue Jesus's work in destroying that, which the devil has done. By so doing, we not only are obedient to our commission, but also advance the Gospel message.

Does it bother you that I said we must take it upon ourselves? Do you feel that "only God can decide who shall minister and who shall not"? In the statement "many are called, but few are chosen" do you not realize that you can better your chances at being chosen by submitting yourself to the training? Think long and hard about that. Once again let's use a sports example.

Perhaps you desire to play on a baseball team. Would you not work hard to become proficient at baseball? The harder you work to improve your baseball skills, the better your chances of being chosen for the team. It is no different with the choice to minister. If you will conduct yourself in a manner that makes you better suited for the choosing, then you have bettered your chances of being chosen. Do you not know that Paul the Apostle said the same thing? In Second Timothy Chapter 2 verses 20 and 21, Paul says,

> "In a large house there are articles not only of gold and silver, but also of wood and clay; some are for noble purposes and some for ignoble. If a man cleanses himself from the latter, he will be an instrument for noble purposes, made holy, useful to the Master and prepared to do any good work."

He placed the impetus on the man to cleanse himself of ignoble things. Furthermore, the result of that purification is being made holy, useful and prepared for *any* good work. As further evidence, please look at Chapter 1 of Second Timothy, verse 6. Paul writes,

> "For this reason I remind you to fan into flame the gift of God, which is in you

through the laying on of my hands."

He places the responsibility on us (read - Timothy) to encourage ourselves in the ministry. And what about Peter? Shall we consider Second Peter chapter 1 verses 5 through 8?

"For this very reason, make every effort to add to your faith goodness, and to goodness, knowledge; and to knowledge, self control; and to self control, perseverance; and to perseverance, godliness; and to godliness, brotherly kindness; and to brotherly kindness, love. For if you possess these qualities in increasing measure, they will keep you from being ineffective and unproductive in your knowledge of our Lord Jesus Christ".

Peter clearly places the responsibility upon our selves to do what the list says.

Perhaps that is too controversial? Well, controversy aside, may we continue upon this previously assumed path? Sickness, death, etc. remains here on earth after the life and sacrifice of Jesus of Nazareth for our training. How do we get trained? Every man's training is different, but it all begins the same. You must want it! Do not hesitate to "enlist" in the army of God. Do you not realize that any man can be trained in some facet of warfare, simply by joining the armed forces? Yet not all members of the armed forces are infantrymen carrying rifles and hand grenades. All service members, be they combat forces, support, or maintenance, have one thing in common: they volunteered. Thus we must also volunteer.

Do not think for an instant that the armed forces are better at training their volunteers than the Lord will be at training His volunteers! No sir! The Lord, although not always as explicit, is by far a better trainer. And the results of His combat are the benefits of the people. We, as soldiers, may have to attack a sickness or a handicap. Our prevailing means health to whoever was sick or wholeness to the handicapped. Can you not see this? But how can the Lord train us in combat against sickness if sickness didn't exist? Do you see the necessity for sickness to be here? Thus, in order for the Lord to be able to train us in the warfare of righteousness, He had to leave some "enemies" in our land of promise.

BAD THINGS HAPPEN TO PEOPLE, WHETHER THEY ARE GOOD OR BAD, BECAUSE WE NEED TO LEARN TO FIGHT AGAINST THESE ENEMIES WITH SUPERNAT-URAL WEAPONRY. Furthermore, we must learn our positions in this battle. This is NOT as unrealistic as it may seem. Consider college debate teams. They prepare for combat, yet they have no "natural" weapons. And if they DID show up with guns and swords, that doesn't mean they would win the debate. That may only eliminate the competition! The "fight" will be with words and documentation. So too it is with sports. Although the "weaponry" is on a more "natural" scale, the lesson remains intact.

The battle lines are drawn in such a manner that all participants are fully aware of the boundaries. They take the battlefield and wage their limited wars. At the end, one is determined to be the winner. But what good would it serve if the greatest tennis player in the world stepped out onto the football field to join their battle? Can you now see the seriousness of getting trained in combat? Does this also help you understand why tennis players practice (read "train in warfare") against other tennis players, and football players train against other football players? Thus, if our warfare is to be against the enemies of man—the four, six and two—then do we not need to train against these enemies? Now you see their importance, and the reason bad things happen to good people.

No training regimen is easy. Oh, I imagine that, with time and practice, it becomes easier. If you decided to get back in shape, physically, you would find the going quite tough. Not only the physical aspects of weight training and aerobics, but the mental aspects as well. For some reason, our minds can always come up with a reason to skip today's workout.

Difficult training results in soreness. Expect it. If you join the local gym, you would expect to be sore the morning after a good, intense workout. Hopefully that wouldn't be enough to make you change your mind about gym membership. Consider for a moment how many millions of people subject themselves to intense physical training everyday in America. For what reason? A body! Whether they seek muscle tone, or mass or shape, they work hard to affect change on their physical body. How much more so should we, as Christians and servants of the Most High God, subject ourselves to the rigors of training for spiritual combat! Hopefully, we will undergo our intense training and not whine to our brethren in so doing.

Expect resistance. Man's enemies don't WANT us to prevail! Our friends, relatives, and even some of our pastors will tell us we have gone off the deep end. Entire denominations will condemn us for insisting that what Jesus said in 30 ad applies to us today. Social organizations will call us right wing zealots, bigots, nuts and extremists. Can you join in the training, and handle the slurs levied against you? This is not an obtuse question. Please consider Jesus's remarks concerning the man building a tower. Luke 14:28-30

> "Suppose one of you wants to build a tower. Will he not first sit down and estimate the cost to see if he has enough money to complete it? For if he lays the foundation and is not able to finish it, everyone who sees it will ridicule him, saying, 'This fellow began to build and was not able to finish.'"

The agony of failure in this instance is ridicule. Can you handle the ridicule? Suppose, just for a moment, that you entered into the training and found later that you were simply called, but not chosen. You would be singled out as the poster child of the anti-training groups. Would you have the character to refute them by saying, "I enlisted, but I was not chosen. Others have been chosen, and I fully support them"? Or would you behave as so many others do, and say that your condition of not having been chosen proves the idea to be fraudulent? The heretic hunters are out there in force. Do you think you would fall prey to them? Do you think that having begun the training, and, hypothetically, dropped out, you could refute the accusations and leanings of the heretic hunters? Don't take offense at that statement because you know deep down inside you that it happens ALL THE TIME! People judge everything by their own personal contact. If it harmed you, it will harm others. If it was good for you, it will be good for others. If someone you greatly respect was injured by the training, then the training must be at fault. You know it is common! I'd like to relate a story to you.

I was working on a counter top with a friend of mine, and we had to mark the area where the stove-top would fit in. He measured the corner points, then laid a level across them as a straightedge. While drawing the line, his hand wavered slightly, resulting in a small "bump" in the straight line. Instantly, and without thinking, he said, "Stupid pencil!" Now I ask you, was the pencil at fault? Of course not, but you can relate to this action from similar situations in your own life, can you not? How many times in your life have you heard something blameless chided for a failure? How many times have you done it yourself? Or I, myself? It happens. Serving the kingdom of

God, as an authorized representative of Jesus of Nazareth is so much more important than our meager lives, that we must realize our own tendencies to deflect blame for failure. It is a part of our considering the cost of the tower. May your tower stand tall and brilliant in the glowing light of the Lord.

I have given you much of my own insight here. Can we apply Scripture here and see if it fits? Please consider Paul the Apostle in First Corinthians 9:24-27—

> Do you not know that in a race all the runners run, but only one gets the prize? Run in such a way as to get the prize. Everyone who competes in the games goes into strict training. They do it to get a crown that will not last; but we do it to get a crown that will last forever. Therefore I do not run like a man running aimlessly; I do not fight like a man beating the air. No, I beat my body and make it my slave so that after I have preached to others, I myself will not be disqualified for the prize.

Win the prize.

It is incumbent upon ourselves to verify all information given to us in the form of godly training. My information is no different. If you are a minister, you owe it to your congregation to examine the reality of this message and to delve even deeper into the Holy Spirit's knowledge. If you are a lay minister, or other type of church worker, you are not exempt. Now that you have heard, you too are expected to search this out in more detail. Your examination will also benefit all around you. If you are not affiliated with the "church" at all, and you only picked this book up for your own personal reasons, the verification of this information is readily available to you in the form of self-research. Get yourself a New International Version of the Holy Bible (available at any Christian book store) and read the passages cited in the book. As you do, the same Holy Spirit that opened my eyes will open yours. That is His duty.

Please understand that it is impossible to force performance. It is equally difficult to perform under pressure. My manifold failures loom before me as gargantuans in the night, yet the knowledge I have received stands stalwart against them. One day, soon I hope, I again will face these enemies, and this time I will prevail.

If you have suffered in such a manner that your predicament urged you to purchase this manual, then you may not have received peace from this work. I hope that between you and the true Author of knowledge, you will find peace. But for the men who have suffered, I hope you find prodding. I hope that your every waking hour is filled with the visions that you can be trained to defeat that which has defeated you. No more people need to suffer permanent trouble if we simply learn to fight. May we learn quickly.

If you believe that you will enlist in the training course, would you pray a very simple prayer? Short and to the point, just ask, "Lord, train me." Then devote yourself to His word and His ways. As you intently study Him, through reading and hearing the word preached, ask that He convert that knowledge to your heart and make you the noble servant that the world needs. You will find that He will accept your plea, and you will begin your courses.

Don't get discouraged! It is imperative to focus and dedicate yourself to the task. Jesus put it this way in Luke 9:62—

Jesus replied, "No one who puts his hand to the plow and looks back is fit for service in the kingdom of God."

If this bothers you, please revisit the portion on the kingdom of God. It is not a disqualification from heaven, but a disqualification from service. And don't read too much into it, either. Consider actually plowing. Would you go to a farm and tend the plow continually? I would think not. Surely one must take a break for lunch. Perhaps stop and get a drink of water. Brief respites from the actual labor are not the same as giving up the job of plowing. It is not as though you (we) would be walking off the farm in disgust, but merely are taking a coffee break before resuming our duties.

If you have found yourself on such a coffee break, then perhaps it is time to get back to work? There is much to do out there in the world, and few (very few) workers to do it. Will you take the job?

Printed in the United States
65450LVS00002B/103-135